LETTERS FROM EGYPT

PIERRE TEILHARD DE CHARDIN

LETTERS FROM EGYPT

1905–1908

PREFACE BY
HENRI DE LUBAC

HERDER AND HERDER

1965
HERDER AND HERDER NEW YORK
232 Madison Avenue, New York 10016

Translated by Mary Ilford.
Original edition: *Lettres d'Égypte. 1905–1908*
(Aubier, Éditions Montaigne, Paris 1963).

LETTERS FROM EGYPT

Preface

Pierre Teilhard de Chardin was born May 1, 1881. On March 20, 1899, he entered the Jesuit novitiate (Lyons province) at Aix-en-Provence, after successful secondary studies at the Mongré school (Villefranche-sur-Saône), followed by some months of mathematics at Clermont-Ferrand. Upon completion of the novitiate, he was sent to Laval, in October 1900, for two years of juniorate, that is, of advanced classical studies. From 1902 to 1905, he did three years of philosophy on the Isle of Jersey, where the scholasticate had just taken refuge following the expulsion laws promulgated by the Combes ministry. In the summer of 1905 he received his assignment for Cairo.

The Society of Jesus is a missionary order. The four Jesuit provinces of France were then (they still are) responsible for important missions in different parts of the world. Those entrusted to the Lyons province were three missions in the Middle East: Armenia, Syria and Egypt. The Egyptian mission ran two big secondary schools, the St. Francis Xavier school in Alexandria (which was closed after the 1914–1918 war, at the time when the Algiers school opened), and the Holy Family school in Cairo. Pierre Teilhard was appointed to the Cairo school as a teacher of physics and chemistry.

He was to stay there three years. Most young Jesuits thus do a period of "regency" in a school of the order, between the periods of philosophy and theology. The letters which Pierre regularly wrote to his parents during those three years have been preserved in his family—like many others, both earlier and later. They con-

7

stitute a homogeneous whole, making it possible to follow the young religious, so to speak, from day to day in his dual capacity of teacher and seeker; for his vocation as a seeker was already evident, and the Cairo area offered him manifold scope in this regard.

This correspondence from Egypt includes sixty-eight letters. They were provided us by Mr. Joseph Teilhard de Chardin, a younger brother of Pierre, and by two of his nephews, Messrs. Régis and Bernard Teilhard de Chardin, whom it is now our pleasure to thank here. Father Auguste Demoment was responsible for the typing; he carefully checked the copy against the original.

Rather than make a selection, we thought it preferable to publish all the letters.[1] As Newman once said, the publication of letters is the real way not only of promoting interest in a biography, but also of penetrating to the heart of things. We are assured, in advance, that the reader will share Newman's view; being eager to know more about the man whose work has given rise to so much study and discussion, he will not reproach us for having taken advantage of his patience. Of course, to penetrate to the heart of things, these letters alone are far from sufficient. The man who wrote them was still very young; Pierre was between 23 and 25 years old. And although he speaks to his father and mother with all the trustingness of a loving son, his tone, understandably enough, is marked by a greater reserve than it would have been in confidences to his brothers. Nevertheless, there is an admirable appositeness and simplicity about it.

The literary talent apparent in the *Lettres de guerre* and the *Lettres de voyage* (*Letters from a Traveller*) is already beginning to take shape in these *Letters from Egypt*. Whatever the

---

[1] All we have done, for reasons of discretion, is to suppress a few sentences relating to third parties; these deletions would amount to about two pages of the present volume, and have nothing to do with Father Teilhard. With the collaboration of Father Demoment, we have added a few brief notes which we felt would clarify the text.

subject treated—scenes of school life or Moslem life, word pictures of the city or desert, reports of geological expeditions, natural history descriptions—the delineation is always firm, the wording precise. All this is the product of a curiosity always on the alert, a curiosity supported by a marvelous keenness of vision. Just as in Claudel's *Connaissance de l'Est* poetry acquires a kind of scientific precision from the meticulous accuracy of the description, so with Teilhard, sometimes even in this early period, scientific description by a similar process blossoms into poetry. Another comparison is in order; these letters are a fitting sequel to, and more perfectly authentic than, the famous *Lettres édifiantes et curieuses* of the early Jesuit missionaries; the spontaneous renewal of a literary genre which has been con-sistently successful for three centuries.

The young "lecturer in physics and chemistry," "museum curator," "assistant to the church administrator"—these are his official titles in the records of the Holy Family school—dedicated himself completely to the work assigned to him from the very first day. He loved his Egyptian students, and his students loved him; several of them attached themselves to him and subse-quently, in different circumstances, gave proof of their loyalty. His letters, written without preparation but not without care, show him to have been infinitely more concerned with science than with literature; the little daily events of school life occupied his mind more than problems of world politics, and he took a keener interest in observing nature than in observing society. Much later he was to recall what for him constituted the "wonders of Egypt": "The East perceived and avidly 'imbibed,' not at all from the point of view of its peoples and their history (as yet without interest for me), but in its light, its vegetation, its fauna and its deserts."

But his specific traits are already apparent. Already one can see very clearly that "passionate love for the universe" which characterized him and with which carping critics have reproached

9

him, without understanding its nature. Nevertheless, in Cairo Pierre Teilhard de Chardin had not yet completely found himself. He had not yet reached the stage of the *Genèse d'une pensée*. But, in addition to the freshness of youth which they exhale, these letters to his parents show us certain qualities which he was to retain permanently: an unaffected gravity, a smiling objectivity, and the "graciousness" of a being as modest and as good as he was magnificently gifted.

HENRI DE LUBAC S.J.

1

SS *Congo,* August 18, 1905

Dear Father and Mother,

The passage affords one leisure, and since all we can see now is some of the precipitous islets around Sardinia, this is a good time to begin this letter to you, which I shall mail from Alexandria.

Well, this is the first day of a delightful passage, and I never weary of watching the opaque blue water, which the steamer cleaves as if it were jelly.

To begin at the beginning, I spent a very peaceful Wednesday in Marseilles. The only place I did not know was the abbey of St. Victor, but I could not get to see it. So I spent the time seeing the Fathers and going to the station to meet my companions; as a result, I learned my way about the streets of Marseilles—not a very difficult feat, but useful, since we often travel through the city.

By Thursday, everyone had arrived, and we spent a rather happy morning, taken up with the final preparations. We went up to Notre-Dame de la Garde, where I naturally did not forget to pray for you. Up there one can see the mountains overlooking Aix, especially the "Pilon du Roi," and it was fun identifying them.[1] I reached la Jolliette at about 3 p.m. after providing myself with the cap which is a must on a sea trip. The *Congo* is a good-sized steamer, much bigger than you might imagine from the postcard I sent you. Alongside it was the Constantinople packet, overcrowded with a pilgrimage to the Holy Land; it left five minutes before we did. The *Congo,* by contrast, carries a very small complement of passengers (among them the Maronite Archbishop of Damascus); and the presence of Father Cattin, superior of our houses in Syria and Beirut, warrants us special consideration.

There are four of us in a very nice cabin, and my first night was as restful as possible in the cot where I perch. As we are four old friends, you may be sure we had a lot of fun. Yesterday, for instance, the sea burst in through a porthole, but the leak was quickly repaired thanks to the willingness of members of the crew, all of them born and bred in Marseilles, and consequently just as obliging as anyone could be.

Now for the trip itself, so far. We left at about 5 p.m. yesterday, and for some time hugged the great rocky cliffs which form the coastline from Marseilles; they are completely white, except for occasional large reddish strata. On account of dinner, we missed the sunset; when we came up again, all we could see was a string of beacon lights; we had passed Toulon. When we woke up this morning, we were out at sea, but a sea even gentler than the day before, in splendid sunlight. The sun rays made it impossible to distinguish Corsica, which only later came into view, with its magnificent mountains. At about 10 a.m. we passed the Straits of Bonifacio. On our left, then, is the long, bare range of Corsican peaks, disappearing in the clouds, and sloping down to a great limestone plateau, whose cliffs, worn

[1] Pierre Teilhard de Chardin had done his novitiate at Aix-en-Provence. The "Pilon du Roi" (King's Rammer") was one of the novices' regular excursion goals. See *Auguste Valensin,* Paris 1961, 25.

12

down by the waves like the one at Etretat, drop a sheer 125 yards into the water. This is where Bonifacio perches; you would think it would come sliding down into the sea at the first earth tremor. On our right is Sardinia, lower, but also bristling with bare, white peaks. What is particularly striking is the absolutely arid character of those countries. That is also their charm. Between the two large islands are a mass of reefs, in particular the Lipari Islands, with their cemetery for the sailors and soldiers of the *Semillante,* which went down as it was leaving for Sebastopol. There are quite a few marine birds in the straits —petrels and loons of a kind which I could not identify.

A Macroglossa stellatorum and a big pyralis with brown markings turned up on the steamer.

We continued past Sardina, and now (3 p.m.) all I can see through the portholes is the indigo-colored sea.

There is virtually no seasickness on board.

There is nothing in sight, neither porpoises (we shall come to those, apparently, after Messina), nor boats.

The next land we shall see will be Stromboli and the Lipari Islands, tomorrow morning.

Saturday, 9 a.m. The Liparis are in front of us now, terribly sheer, rising out of a sea bed between 2,500 and 5,000 yards deep, over which we have been sailing since yesterday. It is very easy to see that they are former volcanoes. We shall very shortly be passing near Stromboli.

The passage continues to be delightful. Not a trace of a swell; just a warmer breeze which warns us that we are moving south.

There are more ships to be seen. When I went up on deck again yesterday, after writing to you, I saw a pretty little white sail boat and a fine black freighter pass quite close by. We have just overtaken a steamer, and another is quite near.

I saw another grey noctua on board, but could not catch it; I do not think we brought it here.

13

Last evening, standing in the bow, we saw a magnificent sunset; the sea was a phosphorescent purple.

3:15 p.m. It's getting rougher; we have just left the enchanting Strait of Messina. Before reaching it, we had sailed through the Liparis, which I was telling you about this morning. On our left is Stromboli—a great cone which now and again belches out clouds of black smoke. At night, apparently, one can see the red lava flowing. Apart from Stromboli and one or two islands like the one I described above, many of the Liparis reminded me of the mountains of Auvergne, though a little steeper: particularly the Chopine or Vache peaks, with great white fissures. This is preeminently the land of fine pumice-stone.

From time to time, along the shore, you see villages with light-green groves. Now we are three steamers following each other; we have overtaken the other two. Sicily is coming into view on our right. Since lunch, the view has become more and more interesting. I went as far forward as possible. Italy and Sicily seem to meet, the former bounded by huge cliffs, the latter with flatter shores, but which rise uninterruptedly into a chaos of very high, cloud-covered mountains. Boats with lovely triangular sails, and a curiously rigged schooner are passing quite close to us, and the steamer brings some flying fish to the surface, all tinged with blue, slipping for long periods over the waves, their fins spread out like sandpipers' wings.

A sudden turn brings us into a strait which comes into view at the last moment, between the sandbank of Charybdis, equipped with a lighthouse, and the rock of Scylla (Italy), where a lovely house now stands. The strait is not wide; one would be able to distinguish men on either shore. On both sides, at the water's edge, the whole area is green with orange and mulberry trees, interspersed with towns of yellow, flat-roofed houses, and then, every half-mile, wide river beds, completely dried up,

14

forming long yellow bands descending from the mountains. These mountains are quite high and absolutely barren, and the least drop of water must be swept down immediately.

Between Messina and Reggio we can see the big steam ferry passing; it transports whole trains.

The view remains unchanged: great barren plateaux in Italy, high mountain ridges in Sicily. Unfortunately, Sicily is somewhat covered with clouds, and the sun is in our eyes; we cannot see Etna. Anyway, a sudden change of course has caused us to turn our backs on Etna, and now we are skirting a part of southern Italy. Rounded ridges descend gently, fanning out to the everlasting green zone of the coast. I can hear the waves breaking over the sides of the steamer, which is normal. The Adriatic passage is always rougher. I shall leave you to go up on deck again. Tomorrow I shall not have much to tell you about except the passengers, because apart from Crete we shall see only water around us.

Sunday, 3 p.m. Actually, there is nothing around us. For some time, yesterday, we continued to round the southern tip of Italy, which is horribly rocky and dried up. The sea had become rougher, and the portholes had to be closed on one side—not ours, luckily, for the cabins warm up very fast.

This morning we passed two small steamers; I could not make out their names, for lack of field-glasses. Gradually the sea became absolutely oily, and the steamer seemed to be cutting a blue mirror rendered iridescent by the sunlight, like watered silk. At one point I distinctly saw a small water spout on the horizon; it looked like a black thread, slightly conical in shape; the doctor to whom I showed it seemed to regard it as a fairly ordinary phenomenon. It rapidly dissolved in a storm which blew up a long way away. I should mention the sudden appearance of a little bird, about the size of a sparrow, which vanished in the rigging. Yet we are a long way from land.

15

Greece is not even within sight. The seas are rather heavier now. We passed a big white packet at some distance; it was probably coming from the Far East. The odd thing is the absence of any animal life; since Messina, not a bird to be seen, and not more than a couple of tunny fish leaping out of the water.

We expected to see the boat from Alexandria, but none has passed so far.

This morning, we had a public Mass on board. On Friday and Saturday, we had had Mass in a cabin. For today, an altar had been set up in what is still called the "battery," and four Masses were celebrated in succession, two in the Maronite rite. The latter were attended by a good number of passengers and by the captain—a particularly distinguished looking man.

As to the passengers, they are divided into four classes. The first class in not numerous and, apart from meals, merges with the second, to which we belong. The foreign element definitely preponderates, and it irks me, as I cross the deck, to hear at least three or four languages being spoken of which I know none.

I should mention the annoying presence of two little Portuguese urchins, no taller than our knees, with yellow faces and inexpressive eyes, whose yells and wild chases draw down upon them the concentrated wrath of the passengers. They have thought up the interesting game of calling to each other at the tops of their voices through the speaking tubes from one deck to the other.

The fourth class is the most interesting, made up of a swarm of Arabs penned up in the bows, where they eat and live after their own manner. On the whole, they seem to be good folk. One of them, a Maronite giant with a fine face, whom I had seen yesterday garbed entirely in Turkish fashion, turned up today, in honor of Sunday, in a grey suit and a Panama hat.

I have just been to see the engines; they are not new, but powerful, and this was the first time I had seen any.

Tomorrow we shall see Crete.

16

Monday, 4 p.m. It has been very calm today. The seas were quite heavy last night, but then subsided, at least so far, and the voyage continues almost without incident other than the very occasional passage of some steamer. When I went up on deck this morning, I saw in the mist the outline of a part of Crete, but not for long, and not distinctly. That will have to keep for another voyage. Two wagtails followed us for some time; I wonder how they can go so far with their erratic flight. It is getting hotter, but it is still quite bearable. Tomorrow, at about 8 o'clock, we shall arrive at Alexandria. I don't know whether I have something of the sailor in my veins, but I never tire of seeing only water; not everyone on board feels the same way.

Tuesday, 3:30 p.m. I am writing to you from Alexandria, which we reached this morning, at 10 o'clock. I am dazzled by everything I have seen in the past few hours, and I am surprised anew each time I look out of a window and see, above the square houses, gilded in a magnificent light, great palm trees laden with green dates.

The last hours of the passage were delightful. Two or three hours before we arrived, a hoopoe came and perched on the deck, and I saw another one in the harbor. The entrance to the port is very beautiful. To the right lies the low, white coast, tapering off to the horizon into the desert, intersected here and there only by a few clumps of palm trees. To the left, a big breakwater and the great lighthouse; in between a multitude of boats, steamers and sail boats with strange riggings.

We were assailed, as is customary, by a flotilla of little boats —motor launches, little boats with triangular sails manned by Arabs of all kinds.

Some other time I shall be able to describe all these fellows whom it is great fun to see in real life after seeing them so often in pictures.

I happened to see an Arab funeral; there is nothing gloomy about it, despite the weepers.

17

I have found my very good friend de Bélinay[1] here. He has just shown me the natural history collection he is assembling—shells, minerals, scorpions, snakes, etc. It is fascinating being in an exotic land like this. I saw a live lizard from Lake Mariut—large, light brown, and flecked with red; and a live varanian lizard from the Nile, measuring at least 20 in.

I think I am going to have a very good time as far as natural history is concerned.

I shall end this letter here so as to get it off quickly. I don't know yet when I leave for Cairo, but I shall write to you very soon. As regards your letters, it doesn't matter what day you mail them, since the postal service routes them not only via Marseilles, but via English and Italian lines. You know my address: Holy Family School, Cairo.[2]

It is quite hot, but it does not bother me.

Goodbye, dear Father and Mother, I kiss you, as well as Guiguite[3] and the boys; you know how much I love you and pray for you all to our Lord. It was very good seeing each other again.

Pierre

---

[1] Father Frédéric de Bélinay (1875–1958) was to found the Jesuit mission in the Chad which now comprises the two dioceses of Fort Lamy and Fort Archambault; his writings include articles on the Chad published in Études, 1938 and 1939.

[2] The Holy Family School still exists in Cairo, directed by the Jesuits.

[3] His sister Marguerite-Marie (1883–1936). She suffered from Pott's disease, and from 1927 was to direct the Union catholique des malades (Catholic Association of the Sick). A collection of her articles in the Trait d'Union was published after her death, with some reminiscences: Marguerite-Marie Teilhard de Chardin, L'énergie spirituelle de la souffrance (The Spiritual Power of Suffering), writings and reminiscences presented by Monique Givelet, preface by Pierre Teilhard de Chardin (Éditions du Seuil, Paris 1951). Like most members of her family, she was an enthusiastic entomologist.

2

Collège
Saint-François-Xavier
dirigé par
les PP. de la Compagnie
de Jésus

Alexandria, August 26, 1905

Dear Father and Mother,

As you see, I am still in Alexandria. The Cairo fathers are making their retreat in the country here, and I am waiting for them so that we can travel together up the bit of the Nile which separates me from my permanent residence. Anyway, I am very luckly to be able to look around Alexandria, which is a curious city, though nothing compared with Cairo, so I am told.

As you know, and as you can see from the sketch on the other side of the sheet, Alexandria stands on a strip of land between the sea and the great lagoon of Mariut, which is very slowly being reclaimed. I find it much more Arab in character than I would have expected. Even the beautiful sections in the center of the city have something Arabic about them, with their terraced houses, drivers in tarbooshes and Arabs strolling about. All around these European sections are the Arab sections, still full of local color. Rows of little shops line the narrow streets, with their overhanging houses; they are grouped according to their trades—fruit venders, cloth merchants, cafés, etc.—without fear of competition. Everything takes place outside, and you have only to take a peaceful stroll through this market (or *"souks"*) to see how shoes are made, or Arab nougat, and many other things.

As for the people, a lot of them are dressed in European style, and still more are Egyptians complete with moustaches, jackets and red tarbooshes (like the khedive); finally there is a milling crowd of Arabs, Jews and a few Negroes. These Arabs really have an incomparably dignified bearing.

My walks through the city have given me, I think, a fairly complete idea of Alexandria. To the west, I have been as far as Mex. That is where all the evil-smelling activities have been relegated; rows of tanneries and slaughter-houses stand rather sadly in the midst of the white sand, as well as long quarries which are worked for a poor species of calcareous tufa, the only local stone, which is used in all construction. A succession of flat carts, sometimes used as buses for the Arab women, serve as the means of transportation along the bumpy roads, among clouds of dust. This is the country of dust; imagine, not a drop of water falls eight months out of the twelve. A little tram brings us as far as Mex, between a small, disused casino and the ruins of one of Mehemet Ali's forts.

Further on, along the shore, there are a few houses, and then sand with occasional palm trees; that is real desert, all the way to Tunisia. From time to time Bedouins come from there on their camels; the road leads under a vaulted gate where a customs officer pierces the huge sacks loaded on the camels' backs with an iron rod. I saw several lines of camels pass, swaying from side to side, with their inane expression.

That is where I had my first swim in the Mediterranean, in water that was positively lukewarm.

After Mex, I went in the direction of Abukir, as far as the khedive's mother's palace. Whereas Mex is mostly Arab, without a single villa, this section is covered with country houses, and more are going up all the time. In fact, so much building is going on that whole areas along the seashore look like construction yards. It's an unpleasant phase that has to be put up with; but this part of Alexandria can become delightful once gardens are fairly intelligently laid out. The sea is very beautiful, and often rough. The beaches, unfortunately, are often dirty, the tides uncovering barely 15 to 25 yards at best. The first evening, I saw the "green ray." The last glimmer of sunlight distinctly appears watery green. It is a phenomenon which cannot, I believe, be explained by strain of the retina, since at that point the light is very soft.

After going west and east, I went north, to the port. There is an excellent lifeboat at the students' disposal, and we spent some pleasant hours rowing among the steamers and the mass of fishing boats or small yachts. We rowed out to the lighthouse, which is very beautiful, built not far from the famous Pharaohs of ancient times—the first of its kind.

But my strangest excusion was to the south. By contrast with the shore route out of Alexandria, which is very long, the route by way of Mariut is very short. I followed a canal which more or less skirts Mariut, and there really caught a glimpse of Arab life. From time to time, a wretched ferry transports the natives, and even a few Arab ladies and their retinues returning to the barred palaces which are not uncommon in that area. Women were coming from all sides to draw water, with the movements of a Rebecca, and men were saying their prayers facing Mecca, the direction of which is carefully located. On the opposite bank —a kind of dam, beyond which lie Mariut and the big maize or sugar cane fields of the Delta, stretching out as far as the eye can see—the native cattle roam: light russet cows, slightly humped, like zebus, and above all *gamoosas* (a kind of "buffalette," so to speak), their big horns folded back, their hides black and shining, wallowing in the mud to their hearts' content. As night falls very fast, I was lucky to go through a large copse of tall date palms just at twilight, and it was a truly exotic pleasure.

Since Tuesday, then, time has passed very quickly. When I am not out, I help my friend de Bélinay organize his museum here. He specializes in conchology, and what I studied this year in Jersey has made me doubly appreciative of the riches of the Mediterranean, though they, in turn, are nothing compared with the treasures of the Red Sea. I have also seen the collections of a father who specializes in insects, and I shall write a separate letter about this to the boys and Guiguite. At the moment I am breeding a batch of caterpillars (from Lycanea, I believe), which devour mimosa pods. In Cairo, I shall have much better facilities than here for identifying species and obtaining all kinds of information.

One thing about Alexandria which would interest Father very much are the horses, which are a favorite luxury here. I chanced upon a whole stableful of horses out exercising; there were at least fifteen or twenty beautiful little horses, stepping in single file (like everything here). At the head of the line, and bringing up the rear, were the men in charge of the stable, looking dignified and bored; between them were a number of colorfully attired and more enthusiastic native riders. It was a curious scene.

The house here has a fine garden; there are still a lot of trees whose names I don't know. I shall mention at least the palm, the banyan, covered with little figs, and the sycamore, also laden with little fruits the size of marbles which grow in clusters along the thick branches. There are also some rubber trees. They are all very tall trees, inhabited and pillaged by a swarm of turtle doves with breasts flecked with brown. Along the shore you see nets spread for passing quails and hoopoes, and in the port quantities of crates in which they are packed and sent off. Thanks to the English, the nets are becoming less and less frequent, and may be spread only at certain spots which for some reason or other enjoy this privilege.

I am now continuing my letter on Monday, the 27th. Last evening I went to the banks of Lake Mariut. The canal was teeming with boats laden with cotton, which is the big item of speculation here. The lake shores are quite pretty, surrounded by marshes and fields of maize and sugar cane. Apparently it is nowhere over a yard in depth. A host of small flat-bottomed boats put out to catch a small fish something like a perch (but it isn't, since the water is brackish). I understand that a little further from Alexandria there are great flocks of half-tame flamingoes—perhaps I shall see some from the train when we cross the Delta.

It is very hot and humid. Fortunately, there is always a pleasant north wind in which one can cool off provided one is exposed to it; the evenings are very pleasant. Altogether, I do not think I shall find it difficult to get acclimated. I expect to be in Cairo about the middle of this week. I shall write you from there.

Goodbye, dear Father and Mother, I kiss you as well as Guiguite and the boys, and I pray hard for you. I haven't received your letters yet, but as you must have addressed them to me in Cairo I expect it's only a delay.

Pierre

3

✠
JHS
Collège
de la Sainte-Famille

Cairo, September 5, 1905

Dear Father and Mother,

My postcard from Matariya will have informed you that I
have finally reached my destination. Now for some more details
about those last few days. Before leaving Alexandria, I went on
another boat trip in the port. It was particularly enjoyable
because some former students who were going by in a fairly
large sail boat took us in tow and led us fast and far. One
certainly misses the sea in Cairo, but there are other advantages.
I left Alexandria in the evening of the 30th, right at the moment
of the eclipse; however little of it remains in view, the sun
out here is bright enough to give off considerable heat and
glare even at the point of maximum occultation. At most, the
plains of Delta were for a time wrapped in weird semi-darkness.

There is nothing so monotonous as this Delta. Once the
brackish coastal lakes are passed, all one sees, stretching on and
on, are endless green fields, flat as the palm of one's hand,

intersected by hedges of trees. One has to remember that these are cotton fields, that the tree hedges have palms among them, and that the spires in the distance are minarets, not steeples, to realize that this is Egypt. Apart from the camels and *gamoosas,* there is only one very distinctive feature: the villages, consisting of accumulations of cubes or hemispheres of dried mud, emerging here and there rather—if I may use the expression— like cow patches in a meadow. And from time to time one sees the tall stacks of the cotton mills.

The express trains (there are many of them, and they travel very fast) pass through this countryside at breakneck speed, and in a cloud of dust which makes the trip very tiring. The carriages have corridors, and are well ventilated, but the dust comes in together with the air; my cassock was grey. An uninterrupted stream of Arabs goes by, selling newspapers, grapes, mangoes. After 3¼ hours, the train arrives in Cairo.

The school is quite close to the station, and the railroad which you can just make out in the photograph I left you is the little Matariya line, separated at that point from the main lines only by a canal.

I haven't been around much yet. First of all, it is hot; secondly, here I am not just in transit, and I shall have plenty of time to enjoy Cairo in the winter; and finally, I have to think of my class and organize the physics apparatus and the laboratory— they need it badly.

In one of my letters I shall send you some sort of plan of Cairo. Cairo lies on the right bank of the Nile, between the river, which is mostly outside, and the Mokattam hills, a great rocky ridge overlooking the city, and on which the Citadel stands. From this point on, the Nile valley with its sugar and cotton fields contracts sharply, and on either side one can see the whitish edges of the desert.

The city itself is very picturesque. The European sections,

25

incredibly luxurious, and intersected by great shady avenues of rubber and eucalyptus trees, are submerged in a completely Arab city. I have not yet seen the bazaars or the great Moslem university, but the forest of minarets visible from our terrace gives one a good idea what to expect.

Yesterday, however, I paid a very superficial and general visit to the big Maspero museum. Although archeology is not my special line, I think I shall often go back there. These Egyptian antiquities are really entrancing, and from a purely esthetic point of view there are some marvels among them. But I shall tell you about that at length and in detail. From our terrace, again, I have seen the Pyramids; I expect to go take a closer look at them very soon.

It is hot here, hotter perhaps than at Alexandria, but the air is dry and the nights are cool. So the climate does not trouble me. In any case, this is the end of summer.

Cairo, you know, is full of kites; you can see them everywhere, and very close to, wheeling near windows, perching on corners of terraces and flagpoles. Apparently, they steal the nests of the hooded crows in the trees in our garden; these crows, apart from swallows, are almost the only birds I have seen here. Our garden is small, but the Matariya countryside is pleasant, with all kinds of trees, particularly huge bamboos. I have been there twice. There were Danais (I believe) on the flowers; they are a kind of vanessa butterfly which is certainly among the exotic ones of the Sarcenat collection. Its wings are uniformly tan, except at the edge and the angle, which are dark, with white spots.

Goodbye, dear Father and Mother; you know how much I love you and pray for you, and Guiguite and the boys too. Since they will read this letter, I am not so sorry about not writing to them; but it is taking me longer to organize things than I thought. I expect you have received all my letters. Apart from the postcard, I have written to you twice before today; one letter describing the sea voyage, the other my stay in Alexandria.

I kiss you.

Pierre

4

Cairo, September 18, 1905

Dear Father and Mother,

I expect you know, now, what Biel[1] is going to do, and I wish I did too; but I suppose I shall have to wait another week for that. I am up to Father's letter of the 10th, which arrived yesterday. I have also received Mother's and Guiguite's letters. Thank you. All these letters give me even greater pleasure here than in Jersey.

The next time I write to you, I shall be very close to my first class; but before that will come the 27th, and I must tell you right now what you already know—how much I shall be thinking of you on that day. This is Albéric's birthday, isn't it, and I shall ask him to help me this year. He will bless your older children, and your younger ones too.

To come back to my class, my functions have now been clearly defined: I am to teach physics and chemistry to the classes corresponding here to third,[2] humanities, rhetoric and philosophy. I say "corresponding" because actually the only thing in common between what goes on here and in the other schools, even that of Alexandria, is the name. This is on account of the

[1] His younger brother Gabriel, sixth of the eleven children in the family. Pierre was the fourth.
[2] Corresponding approximately to second-year high school—tr.

28

preparatory studies for the Egyptian examination, which requires Arabic, French, English, history and mathematics, but neither Latin nor Greek. The humanities' teacher, for instance, chiefly teaches French grammar, and I doubt that it is much different in rhetoric. The examination is in two parts: one part is taken after the humanities and is prepared in third and in humanities; the other is take after philosophy and is prepared in rhetoric and philosophy. This examination *entitles* the graduate to a state-remunerated position, and the pay here is good. So there is considerable inducement.

As for me, my program is quite a humble one; my chief difficulty will be to work out and grade my classes, to correct homework, etc. I foresee that these years are going to be a valuable exercise in imagination and judgment for me. Say a prayer to Notre Dame du Port that all may go well.

The students are very nice; they keep coming to the school, and I have to withdraw rather so as not to lose my prestige in the familiarity of vacation time. A few months from now I shall not have to fear this disadvantage any more. But first they have to know me as a teacher. Anyway, I shall have all year to tell you about these interesting characters.

Now for some details about Cairo, which I have explored more than I had expected to. You can follow my trips on the enclosed map.

1. Boulak Island. This is a pleasure spot. A little steam ferry, operating about a half-mile below the bridge of Kasr-al-Nil, brought me right to the gardens of the Gezira mansion (Gezira means "island") which Mehemet Ali built for the Empress Eugenia; now it is an ordinary hotel. The gardens, which are very beautiful, and embellished (?) with grottoes and rockeries (the slabs are madreporic rocks from the Red Sea, and the benches trunks from the silicified forests of the desert), were unfortunately just in process of being planted. But at least there were the trees, among which I noticed several clumps of

Solanaceae, the size of "Françoise's tree" at Sarcenat, and covered with big purple flowers, very typical of the kind. The island is almost entirely surrounded by a magnificent walk shaded by enormous lebbek acacias which forms a loop around the race course. Apparently the left branch of the Nile, which is very narrow, and immediately beyond which the cotton fields start, is almost dry in winter. The river flows almost entirely to the right. Now (we are right in the flood period), the water is reddish and absolutely opaque, and lines of *dahbyes,* boats with sails like swallows' tails, all built alike, move up and down the river (very fast, thanks to a providential and very constant north wind). It is a fairy-like scene. The aquarium of Nile fish is located in one part of the island. A good many of the species are catfish, or something similar, with long wattles. Two types of splendid red-gold fish deserve mention: the *Malopterurus electricus* (it looks like a catfish), and various small fish with twisted or protruding snout-like mouths.

I returned to Cairo by way of the great Kasr-al-Nil bridge, which is always magnificent in the setting sun. That is the time people drive out in their carriages, and you can see an unbelievable medley of open coaches full of tourists or Englishmen, closed landaus where you can glimpse veiled Mohammedan women, a few cars, and almost always camels, which pass through this crowd (often in a long line) with superb disdain. As I told you, Cairo remains completely Arab in spite of the civilization which has established itself alongside the ancient customs. It is sufficient to take a few steps outside the section of sumptuous mansions to plunge into a maze of narrow streets where few Europeans are to be seen, or none at all. On both sides are overhanging houses with barred balconies, and one passes an uninterrupted series of sidewalk shops where the shopkeeper sleeps as he waits for his customers, or busies himself embroidering tapestries or cutting exquisite jewels. From time to time one passes a serrated mosque. Little paths, along which one can walk only in single file, branch off from the street, which is itself not very wide; here are more bazaars of all kinds, with arcades running from one street to the other. This is what usually impresses newcomers to Cairo most. But I prefer the desert.

2. It was yesterday that I got furthest into the desert. We set out from the Citadel which, as you may know, is occupied by the British. Their barracks, fortunately, are tucked away, and in no way spoil the character of this part of the city, which boasts the most beautiful mosques, one of them Byzantine, surmounted by two interminable, needle-fine minarets. I was with the intrepid Father Garraud[1] who acted as our guide, and my friend, Bovier-Lapierre,[2] an ardent naturalist, with whom I did so much exploring in Jersey three years ago (my first year of philosophy), and who arrived rather unexpectedly in Cairo this week for a stay of at least a year, to my delight. We went by way of the Fort Napoléon, and made a great circular trip into the mountains. It is horribly dry, but completely wild; there is nothing right up to the Red Sea. From time to time, you come to deep ravines carved by the torrential winter rains; at the bottom, there is a river bed still covered with thick-leaved plants of various kinds (which I shall try to describe to you bit by bit), and all around jagged ridges and slopes in which you can clearly see the long seams of sedimentary rock. It reminded me of the illustrations in the big book on the Holy Land at Sarcenat. Though these are not yet high mountains. They are slopes, but so sheer and rocky that it comes to much the same. Twice I saw a bird the size of a thrush, very white, with black wings, head and tail. Perhaps I shall find it again at the Cairo museum. In

[1] Father Victor Garraud (1848–1925), a native of Auvergne, was English instructor at the school.

[2] Father Paul Bovier-Lapierre (1873–1950), science instructor at Cairo and Alexandria, professor of botany and microbiology at the University of St. Joseph in Beirut; he was one of the founders of the Cairo ethnographic museum, and a great friend of Father Teihard.

31

the hollows you see beetles with immense legs running at great speed, like spiders. I also brought back a very small red and black lebia (??), and some large and quite beautiful celestite crystals (sulphate of strontium), of which we identified two beds. Not to speak of all kinds of fossils.

We returned to civilization at the "Tombs of the Caliphs," gazing upon its cupolas and decorations of purest Arab style, etched against the purple sky. The sunsets in this atmosphere replete with dust have extraordinarily warm colors.

3. I must also say a word about a trip I made from Matariya to Marg, a couple of miles further on. When you leave the area around the school, you come to the site of ancient Heliopolis, of which there remains hardly anything more than a magnificent obelisk (of rose granite from Aswan), perhaps the oldest Egyptian monument, and then you plunge into the middle of the plantations of the Nile valley—almost always cotton, with still a few big yellow flowers, but mostly with seeds from which the wadding escapes in beautiful flakes through the cracks in the pods. From time to time one walks under mimosas, lebbek acacias with their rich foliage, and along miry canals where little toads make a racket like castañets. At that spot I saw a flight of green birds with light breasts—bee-eaters or something of the sort.

But the prettiest is Marg itself, surrounded by its forest of date palms. If you have seen photographs of oases in the Sahara, you have only to recall them to know what Marg looks like. Vegetation tapers off gradually and suddenly one is right in the desert, with date palms on all sides, of all ages, in clumps or long avenues, with clearings, and a well devised irrigation system which brings each tree its stream of water. In the midst of all this are the Arabs' huts, camels, natives gathering the heavy clusters, while their children fight or play at the foot of the tree.

There are at least twenty types of date palms in Egypt, with fruits ranging through all the colors, from black to yellow, via red and pink. The yellow ones taste best, and they are the only ones I have tried so far; in taste they are much like those you get in France in boxes. At Matariya I picked some guavas; the tree and the fruit are similar to the quince, at least outwardly. The fruit, stripped of its oily rind, is white, filled with little seeds, and has a faint strawberry aroma.

I shall go on slowly with this description of Egypt, which I like very much, particularly because of its proximity to the real desert. Probably, too, before very long, a good part of my heart will be given over to my youngsters—but I have no experience of that yet.

Goodbye, dear Father and Mother, I kiss you and pray for you and the family. All the best to the boys, for whose benefit I have added some entomological details.

In addition to the insects I mentioned, I caught a big brown click-beetle (as big as our biggest red one, at Mongré).

A kiss to Guiguite.

Pierre

5

Dear Father and Mother,

One unfortunate consequence of our letters' taking a week to arrive is that I am not yet clear as to the circumstances—happy or otherwise—of the boys' return to school. The Centrale[1] lists certainly take a long time coming out . . . Fortunately, you are at least keeping Joseph, and as for poor Gonzague,[2] I shall think of him tomorrow, going off to Jersey. I wonder whether his great regret at leaving Auvergne will not be a little mitigated by the joy of getting back to the sea and seeing his little friends again.

Here the students will begin arriving in force tomorrow evening, but especially on Tuesday morning, since most of them are day boarders. I shall give my first class on Wednesday. My next letter will probably be chiefly about my first impressions of teaching.

I am up to Mother's letter of September 20, in which she tells me of the glorious end of a nyroca duck; I still remember the one Father bought, but too late to stuff, at a fruit vendor's in the rue du Port. I am told that ducks abound in winter in the Delta and on Lake Mariut; I don't know if I shall see any here.

---

[1] *École centrale des arts et manufactures:* a major engineering school—tr.
[2] Joseph was eighth in the family, Gonzague tenth.

Within the past two weeks I have made two more lovely trips to the desert, which I enjoy more and more, as do Father Bovier-Lapierre and Father Garraud, our inseparable guide. You will easily see our approximate itinerary from the map I sent you last time.

We set out from Matariya to explore the Red Mountain. To reach it, one has to cross a sandy plain, marked by occasional saline efflorescences. The mountain itself, which is not very high, and formed of a sedimentary or sandstone rock (consisting solely of accumulated grains of quartz and flint fragments), of a really dark red color, is erratic in contour. It consists of great heaps of broken-up fragments, reminding me—though the heaps here are higher—of the sites of former quarries at Volvic. Here and there a more compact rock stands out, and the whole jagged mass is quite actively quarried.

We returned to Cairo through the winding Mokattam hills, by way of the beautiful tombs of the Caliphs. The region is absolutely barren, traversed by ravines and river beds. In some parts the rock is formed solely of claws of fossil shell-fish, which must have been about the size of lobsters. That is where I found two agamas, one bigger than a hand, the other as long as a finger. That is the one I am rearing. As you see, it is something between a lizard and a chameleon, and looks like a frog with a tail. It is a greyish yellow with dark brown spots and a light, rather flat breast. It blends with the sand and lifts its tail when it runs. I saw another little one last Thursday in the Lybian desert.

That day we made a real excursion. We began by going to the Giza Pyramids, by a very beautiful route. On our way to a ferry a little south of the island of Roda, we passed through a part of Old Cairo, which is very picturesque, with narrow streets bordered by tall lebbeks (they are more like mimosas than acacias, and they have big ball-like flowers). It was still early morning, and the Nile looked lovely, covered with boats and bordered, on the opposite bank, by a screen of palms partially wrapped in mist. The ferry brought us to Giza, and from there a tram took us to the Pyramids.

The Pyramids stand at the edge of the desert, and the desert itself ends abruptly, at a sandy cliff overlooking the Nile valley, often almost perpendicularly. The word "cliff" is particularly apt, since this is the period of full flood, so that on either side of the highway, straight as an i, running from Giza to the Pyramids one sees an indefinite expanse of water. The highway is evidently on a causeway, shaded by the inevitable lebbeks, which were planted by the Empress Eugenia. The water is not deep, so that one can see the tops of occasional cotton plants which have not been picked; it cannot be more than a yard deep, but it goes on as far as the eye can see. At the end of the highway and of the tram line, at the foot of the desert cliff, there is an English hotel, with the proverbial legion of donkey drivers, camel drivers and guides of every kind lying in wait for the tourist. We eluded them easily, but they are really amusing to watch, picking up whatever they can find to offer it in exchange for baksheesh, talking about forty-*one* centuries, and in bad French too.

There are three Pyramids here: that of Cheops, which is gigantic, another almost as big, and a third which is much smaller. They are built of limestone quarried at Tura (near Helwan), which was brought from the other side of the Nile along causeways of which some traces still remain. The casing which covered them has disappeared (except on a part of the second), so that instead of being smooth, they rise in tiers. I did not attempt the ascent, which must be trying rather than difficult. A little to the south of the Pyramids is the Sphinx, carved out of the rock itself, and which is periodically cleared. It really stands lower than the Pyramids, since it is carved in the layer of rock which supports them, and it does not appear large in comparison with them, even though the face is a good thirteen feet high. The sand and the wind have seriously damaged it, but from a distance it retains some expression. Close by is the Temple of the Sphinx, made of very fine granite from Aswan; it was an underground structure, but it has now been uncovered, and can be seen from above.

True enough, there is colossal size here, but, apart from the features of the Sphinx (and they are damaged anyway), there is nothing esthetic about it, unless it be the thought that the Pharaohs were responsible for it. I confess that I enjoyed the rest of the trip, which took up the main part of the day, infinitely more.

As soon as you reach the plateau and the foot of the Pyramids, you are suddenly in the desert, but I noticed this much more during a long circular expedition in the Libyan desert. The impression is stronger than at Mokattam; instead of plateaux intersected by rocky ravines, there is an endless vista of sand slopes rising gradually to a mountainous ridge on the western horizon. In the part where we were, the crests of these wind-swept slopes are covered with big flint pebbles and nodules, often cracked by the heat, which have remained after the sand was swept away. These flints are very distinctive, formed of concentric layers the color of polished walnut. Among them one can find a few agates and a profusion of fragments of silicified wood. As in the Arabian desert, there are many river beds, indicated by a series of fatty plants growing here and there, whose flowers we shall see in a few months' time. The valleys are wide, sloping gently, and at some places quite white with the shells of fossil oysters which, with sea-urchins, cover the rock reefs of this region.

Further north, the slopes seem to become mainly sandy, judging by their whiteness. I certainly intend to continue my explorations in that direction at the next opportunity. As regards animal life, all we saw were some lizards which we were unable to catch, a little owl the size of a sparrow owl, a scorpion which we killed, a small insect identical with a scorpion except that it had no tail, and finally several specimens of a curious coleopterus, shaped like a water beetle, and the same size, which runs at a vertiginous speed and has this distinctive trait, that it is covered with a very delicate old-rose down which makes it blend absolutely with the sand. Near the Pyramids I also found a big black-beetle, its wing sheaths bristling with spikes, which I have certainly seen sketched by Brehm or Acloque.

I understand that there are a good many gazelles and jackals in these deserts.

There must be some horned vipers. As for the *uraens* (haje), I think it is becoming uncommon in the Cairo region; moreover, it likes a little humidity.

As a change from the desert, I made a long trip yesterday between Matariya and the Nile, in the plantations, which are high now. Out there, the flood does not look at all the same as it does around Giza; it takes the form of canals flowing everywhere, and which at most make some of the fields swampy. One can walk along paths between fields of cotton, maize and also sugar cane, which I am beginning not to confuse with maize when both are growing. The cane has a distinctive blue-green color. Here and there great mimosas grow; one meets fellaheen, their donkeys and *gamoosas,* which sometimes fold back their ears with a terrified air. I think this is a good time to go around the fields, which look pleasingly fertile. I believe I placed Matariya west of the Ismailia canal on my map; it was a mistake —I had mixed it up with a secondary canal. The canal is shown correctly, but Matariya is one or two miles to the east (on my paper that would be about a half-inch or an inch to the right, at the same level).

As I was following the earth-bank bordering this canal yesterday, I came across a "pharaoh's rat," or ichneumon. The one I saw was the size of a large cat, more elongated, with a long pointed tail like a rat's, but hairier. Apart from the tail, it was rather like a badger. It ran in front of us for a while, appearing to fear the water of a ditch which it finally jumped over, very neatly incidentally, but somewhat half-heartedly. People sometimes raise it here like a kind of cat.

I have seen two more of the bee-eaters I told you about in my last letter.

I was relieved to find that the local kite is not the royal kite, since it performs the office of a common vulture. Apparently, around the British barracks it comes to take bones from the soldiers' hands. It has a monotonous cry, like the creaking of a wheelbarrow; it has nothing of the wild beauty of the cry of the buzzards which I remember hearing in the Valettes wood, or of the small vulture which I listened to more than once near Aix.

I am closing this letter on Monday, upon receipt of Father's letter of the 25th. It is certainly good, in a way, that Biel should be staying with you a bit longer. You might perhaps pass on this letter to Yéyé,[1] the glorious hunter. At this time the poor little fellow can't be looking forward to going to Paris in the near future.

Yes, it was at my request that my friend de Bélinay sent you the chameleon; I thought you might be able to keep it a few days, long enough to enjoy its transformations. It came from Alexandria. Here, apparently, they are uncommon.

I remember old Father Loradoux very well, and I shall certainly pray for poor Uncle Charles, whom I did not know.

Goodbye, dear Father and Mother, I kiss you, as well as Toto,[2] Biel and Joseph. You know how much I love you and pray for you.

Pierre

[1] His brother Olivier.
[2] His younger brother Victor.

Of course these days all the talk in Cairo has been about the explosion of the *Chatham* and the probable damage to the Suez Canal. At Port Said, apparently, on the morning of the great day, people were camping away from their homes for fear of sharing the fate of the poor Calabrians!

I enclose three stamps for Toto.

6

Dear Father and Mother,

I am late writing to you, but you will have attributed that, correctly, to the hustle of the opening of term. In the past three weeks I have not had much time to myself, which makes the days go by quickly, and is restful in a certain way, but leaves little leisure for writing.

So now I have made contact with the students and with school life. Just before the opening of term I was really rather worried, and now, on the contrary, I am pretty much at home, although I realize much better how difficult it is to make oneself intelligible to children. It is especially when I am with my youngsters in third, thirty-five of them, that I wonder how a truth can penetrate those little heads. One has to strain one's ingenuity to find more or less juvenile ways of presenting things which one is accustomed to considering from a very different angle, and the first few times it is far from easy. But it forces one to clarify ideas which one had thought were quite clear, but which were really only partially so. Of course, I don't know all my students yet, particularly those in humanities and third; most of them have outlandish names which do not correspond to anything our ears are accustomed to. But they are nice youngsters, and I expect that by the end of the year I shall have become attached to them as well as to the big fellows of the upper classes. You would be amused to see me holding forth in front of all these brown—and also white—faces, all so Oriental, and so obviously to be capped by the inevitable tarboosh as soon as school or class is over.

Did I tell you that I was in charge of the altar boys? This way I get to know youngsters who are not in my classes. I shall end up by knowing most of them here, especially on account of the "omnibus." This is a bus which makes two trips every day to pick up and take home some of the day-students, and I have been appointed to supervise the operation. It is really diverting, particularly since each trip represents a good three-quarters of an hour riding all over Cairo. Returning the students is simple; we drop them at their homes. Picking them up is much more colorful. When we arrive in front of a student's house, I blow my whistle once, loudly, and if no one turns up after a reasonable delay we go on, leaving the poor youngster to find some other way of getting to school on time. Sometimes one sees him appear half dressed on a balcony, gesticulating desperately. It is very picturesque, especially inside the vehicle. There are at least fifteen of them, mostly of the seventh, eighth and ninth grades,[1] some of whom remind me of Toto, chattering away and telling me all kinds of stories. Add to that the fascination of driving through the main sections of Cairo morning and evening, and you will see that as far as my bus activities are concerned I am not to be pitied.

Yesterday I received your letter of the 11th. It moved me to realize that Father had written his letter in the big room at Rocquet, and I was interested in what he said about the mountain otters. I shall now be able to prove to Fréd. de

[1] Corresponding approximately to the fourth, fifth and sixth grades in the U.S.—tr.

Bélinay that, in this respect at least, the Couzes are as good as Dordogne.

I have not said anything yet about my joy at Biel's success; it is a great relief to him to see his future more or less completely traced, except for the particular field in which he decides to specialize. I would urge him now to look about him right away to get an idea of the lines which might interest him most. Yéyé must be encouraged to pass next July, and I am happy that he is now among the sophomores.

Two or three days after term opened, I had a very pleasant surprise, owing to the *Chatham*. Taking advantage of the forced stop of their steamer, the group of young Jersey fathers[1] bound for Shanghai came to us from Port Said for two days; I spent some happy hours again, for the last time, with some very good friends who had been my constant companions for five years. I initiated them in all the local curiosities.

For the past three weeks I have not been out except on my weekly excursions to Matariya, where I am going in a few hours, after a bus trip to take the students home for Thursday evening. Last time, we explored what remains of the ruins of Heliopolis. Apart from the obelisk I told you about, nothing remains but some embankments marking (?) the site of the city. At most one finds an occasional fragment of granite, or some slab carved with hieroglyphics or a pharaoh. Certainly if the city were built of mud, as are the buildings of the fellaheen today, nothing much would have remained. Excavations carried on last year uncovered nothing. All along these dusty embankments marking the site of Heliopolis there is a canal, and on the other side a delightful path. By contrast with most others, it is grassy, skirting a date-palm grove, then a big field of banana trees, and is itself shaded by tall mimosas. These mimosas sweat large quantities of a transparent brown gum,

[1] Coming from the Isle of Jersey, where they had studied philosophy with Pierre Teilhard de Chardin.

which is perhaps the original gum-arabic. On their trunks I found a number of laciocampa caterpillers, no more than 1 or 1½ inches long. One of them has already made a little cocoon. This might interest Guiguite, whom I thank very much for her letter of the 12th.

Goodbye, dear Father and Mother, I have to prepare for tomorrow's class. I kiss you and pray for you.

Pierre

7

Dear Father and Mother,

Today and tomorrow are days when I naturally think more about you and about those who are gone, and it is lucky that just now I should have time to write to you. Egypt may not be at the end of the world, but I believe one feels the family's affection here more than ever, and that helps me to pray to our Lord more for you all.

I have just received Mother's letter from Tours, and her good news about the older ones and Françoise[1] makes me very happy; Father wisely foresaw that Françoise would not be sent too far from Tours, and since she is now a mendicant, her dearest wishes have been fulfilled. I remember her telling me about all this in August.

As for Biel, it is good to know that he is happy, and the best sign is that he is satisfied where he is. So our good Joseph is the only one who can call himself unhappy; I hope that he does not think himself too unfortunate, or let himself get demoralized. He has obviously had bad luck, and a year well

[1] Françoise, third in the family, and Pierre's senior, entered the order of the Little Sisters of the Poor; she died, as superior of the Shanghai house, in June 1911. See *Soeur Marie-Albéric du Sacré-Coeur* (Petites Soeurs des Pauvres, Rennes 1914), and *La pensée religieuse du Père Pierre Teilhard de Chardin* (Aubier, Paris 1962), 342–343 and 360–361.

45

spent is never lost. How right you are to keep him until the new year.

Meanwhile, I go on giving my classes, and gradually acquiring the habits of the old teacher which I shall perhaps one day be. What I continue to feel most strongly is that as long as one does not teach, one retains an enormous store of half-digested truths. It is quite hard work clarifying them, but salutary, and I get deep satisfaction from the realization that I learn by teaching. I do not find teaching itself tiring at all, and I really believe that the school is a restful place for me. I am beginning to know my rhetoricians and philosophers; they are fine young people, and quite likable. It is a pleasure to help them, and one would like to do them some good. I hope to have a picture of them around the end of the year, and I shall certainly send it to you.

The biggest event of last week was the khedive's return to Cairo from Europe. As the station is quite close to the school, we saw his train arrive, made up entirely of big yellow cars, and we watched him leave the station to the sounds of a cannon salute. The loveliest thing was his guard, mounted on the beautiful grey Arab horses which are everywhere to be seen here. The khedive's arrival coincides with the arrival of the tourists who fill the sumptuous hotels around the Erbekich gardens throughout the season.

Then Ramadan began. You know that during that season, Moslems do not eat, drink or smoke so long as the sun is above the horizon. This penitential season appears, nevertheless, to cause them great jubilation, and in the evening, from my bus, I can watch the streets swarming with Arabs, and the little children all swinging colored tin lanterns—the shop windows are full of these lanterns.

So the bus has by no means spent its charms for me; now we pass a caravan of camels, laden with great sugar canes (incidentally, I have not tasted sugar cane yet, but I shall certainly do so, if only in memory of the Swiss Family Robinson); now we go by a police station (*caracol*) just at the time when the *gâfirs,* or night watchmen, go on duty, and you feel that you would not like to meet those sinister fellows, all dressed alike in coat and cap of grey homespun, and armed with cudgels.

This week there was a light and brief shower over a part of Cairo; those were the first drops of rain to fall since I arrived. At least the air has cooled off, and we are in the period of mild weather which will go on until the heat starts. Only the mosquitoes never disarm; there are goodness knows how many species of them against which it is war to the death morning and evening.

The school now possesses two young dogs of the Er-man breed (I do not know how to spell it). It comes from Upper Egypt, and is apparently one of the most vicious and stupid breeds known. Their function is to be watchdogs. For the time being they are quite guileless and affectionate, turning up everywhere and everywhere leaving evidence of their passage. They are very interesting, and this is the moment to gain their favor.

Goodbye, dear Father and Mother; tell Gonzague that I was happy to receive his letter; I shall send him at least a postcard when I find an attractive one. Kiss Toto. You know how much I love you.

Pierre

8

Cairo, November 16, 1905

Dear Father and Mother,

I am writing to you as I supervise a composition class, which is not very conducive to gathering one's thoughts.

First of all, I have received all your letters, and thank you for them; now I am waiting daily for a letter announcing the safe arrival of young de Mareschal; perhaps also the death of a woodcock . . . Poor Joseph! He is lucky, though, to have the chance to miss, and I am not surprised that Yéyé should eye his hunting gun longingly.

My life here goes on unchanged; my principal concern is with the experiments and conduct of the next class. But I notice that I am getting used to my role quite quickly, and the difficulties I anticipated are progressively vanishing. Morning and evening I go out in my bus, and one of our latest surprises was to see some Arabs with some kind of dog-faced baboons on the leash, and also some *gâfirs* noisily rounding up a bunch of miscreants whom they had taken in a night raid. Not to speak of the camels laden with sugar cane which pour into the station square. My youngsters' chief delight is to pass a branch of the Galeries Lafayette[1] at night; the name

[1] A department store—tr.

lights up in yellow, red and blue in turn, and they bet end-lessly on the color which will be next to appear—just as Toto would do.

Twice, recently, I have been able to escape with my friend Bovier-Lapierre, and we used the time to explore Marg and its palm forest more thoroughly; I mentioned it to you before. Now all the clusters have been gathered; on the other hand, the undergrowth is drying out as the flood waters withdraw, and one can walk almost freely on a carpet of a sort of light green clover which the fellaheen sow everywhere. Of course, one does not have the impression of being in a forest as one walks among the trunks of the date palms; but it is beautiful never-theless, especially when the trees are young and form something like copses.

To my companion's great joy, and somewhat to mine too, things are beginning to grow; a host of curious plants are emerging all along the canals. One of them, from a distance, looks exactly like wood-sorrel as to the leaves, but it is really a cryptogam (*marsilia(op?)* I believe), its young shoots rising straight up from the extended rhizomes. We eventually arrived at a huge clearing surrounded on three sides by date palms, and opening onto the white dunes of the desert. The clearing itself is taken up for the most part by rice paddies; this gave me my first sight of ripe rice on the stalk. Where the ground is not flooded, it is covered by a light crust of salt deposited by the brackish waters, which creates the very odd impression that one is walking on frosty ground in an African setting. I saw two or three rather small sandpipers, whose song reminded me of Allier gravel. Incidentally, for the past month we have been invaded by wagtails. They seem to be the kind I remember we used to see in the evening as we returned from hunting during the final days of the vacation.

The only interesting animal we came across was a kind of small lizard, which seems to be a cross between the blindworm and the common lizard; it is all shiny, its feet are very small, its tail as thick as its body, and it has a distinctive wriggling motion—it slithered as much as it walked. I shall find out its name eventually. This evening I am going off on another trip to those parts. But what I especially want to see again is the desert. I shall treat myself to a trip there at the new year's vacation.

I have met a French geologist here, Mr. Fourtan, who identifies the local fossils for me. He is a very learned man, but a Gascon through and through, which makes his conversation very amusing. Oddly enough, he quotes Latin at every turn.

Ramadan continues; the funniest thing is the explosion of enthusiasm which greets the evening cannon shot marking the end of the fast. Everyone rushes to the wretched little open-air kitchens whose aroma fills the street corners; someone told me that his driver had once left him for a moment to go to restore his inner man.

We have had some very humid days of fog, but no rain yet, and it is pretty hot.

Goodbye, dear Father and Mother; I kiss you as well as Guiguite, Toto, Joseph. I wrote to Françoise on the occasion of her vows, perhaps a little late. I hope my letter will have been forwarded to Tourcoing. I pray hard for you all.

Pierre

9

Dear Father and Mother,

As last time, my letter will reach you with some delay, but that will not surprise you. I had extra work to do, but it is pretty well finished now; and I think it is better, after all, to work a bit harder than to flunk altogether when it comes to correcting compositions.

Let me tell you, first of all, that I have received the good news of the arrival of Pierre de Mareschal. Please congratulate his parents and grandparents for me, and tell them that I pray for the future happiness of this interesting child with whom I am flattered to have to share my given name. The sight of this little one must reawaken many regrets in your hearts; one just has to keep telling our Lord that his will must be done, doesn't one? But I think of you a great deal.

My life goes on here, very interestingly on the whole, punctuated by one or two weekly outings in the desert. Since my last letter I have been into the Mokattam hills some four times, and I am beginning to find my way about there, which is not easy; though there are no trees, one can easily lose one's way in the midst of these dunes and wadis which are all alike and extend as far as the eye can see. The vegetation there, just now, is at a minimum; the rare green plants which mark the bottom of the ravines have exhausted the supplies of sap stored in their leaves, and are withering. Nevertheless, we have had a little rain this week, and that will be a signal for a (very relative) revival of verdure.

My latest finds, in the desert, are some fossil fish vertebrae the size of 5-franc pieces. I have not had them identified yet. Incidentally, I have met a charming Egyptian, Dr. Iñes Bey, about whom Mr. du Buysson had spoken to me. He has at his home a fairly general collection of all the natural history curiosities of Egypt: shells, coleoptera, lepidoptera . . . and ornithology. I shall examine the latter section especially for Father's benefit. I shall find there the name of the black and white desert birds (which I saw last Sunday at very close range) whose probable name Father sent me two months ago. Here is a more complete description: they are smaller than black-birds, and a beautiful black, except for the top of the head and the lower part of the body (save the tail), which are pure white. In the same rocks, other birds of the same species had completely black heads, and less white on the breast. Is it simply the difference between male and female? A flock of swifts flew by at the time, quite high, incidentally, and whistling as they do at home in July. I also came across a rather curious snake in the desert, between 16 and 20 inches in length, and as thin as a whip lash; it was yellowish grey with brown speckles. I did not manage to kill it; it is distinctive by reason of its incredible thinness. I do not think it was dangerous.

As regards plants, the other day—again in the desert—we came across a crop of small wild squash; the leaves are small, very jagged, and the fruit, which is round and green, is as big as a fist. It is appallingly bitter in taste. My learned companion opined that it was probably *Cucurbita prophetarum.*

Lately my bus has presented me with a surprise more distinguished than monkeys, camels and sugar cane, namely the khedive in person, who went by a few yards away, very dignified under his tarboosh, and escorted by his mounted guard, on magnificent horses, armed with lances with green pennons, and also wearing tarbooshes. The best part of the story is that as soon as the parade of pashas had gone by, my driver attached himself to the rear of the convoy so as to take advantage of the opening, so that in a moment I found myself proceeding, with my enormous old rattletrap, between two rows of respectful Arabs of every condition, who left an enormous space for our passage, ensured by a cordon of police (shaweesh). It was rather embarrassing. Unfortunately, I had not yet picked up any students at the time. They would have been thrilled. Just now they are stirred up about the events in Crete, which coincided with the big celebrations marking the close of Ramadan. Among the news items from abroad, I particularly noted, understandably, the loss of the unfortunate *Hilda,* which I knew well, though it did not stop at Jersey. That called up memories of green sea and rocks covered with algae. I certainly retain deep impressions of that countryside.

I have written to Gonzague, and have tried, incidentally, to persuade him of the merits of his school and of the advantages of more assiduous study. Anyway, his term is drawing to a close, which must cause Joseph a much more tempered joy. However, since he has shot a woodcock, he will be able to leave without regret. Tell him that I enjoyed his letter very much, and that I shall be interested to receive further details about his mineralogical finds.

Goodbye, dear Father and Mother, I kiss you and pray for you all. I shall do so especially on the 8th. All my very best to Guiguite.

Pierre

10

Dear Father and Mother,

This time I believe I am still later in writing than before, though I would have wished this letter to reach you by Christmas. It would be wise, anyway, to wish you now, with all my heart, a happy new year. You know I shall pray to our Lord, asking him to make it a blessed year for you and the rest of the family. I don't need to tell you again that my affection for you remains as great as ever, and causes me to think of you often. I am happy that Yer-Yer is coming to you so early! In addition to his happiness, it will mean a merrier Christmas for you. I expect that if you do not spend it at Vialles, you will leave for Vialles directly after, since the ducks must be allowed a longer respite. Wish Yer-Yer good hunting from me; I believe the wild fowl is beginning to abound in the Delta, but the only indication I have seen of it was a triangle of ducks flying over the house the other day, very high.

I must admit that I do not go to the banks of the Nile much, an omission which I am resolved to remedy; but I still wonder to what extent one can follow those banks, at least while the river is in spate. Now that the waters are abating I shall be able to try. However, the desert has not exhausted its surprises. Last Thursday, as I was going quite far in the

54

direction of Suez, in a terrain strewn with silicified wood, I came across a magnificent vulture tearing a piece of carrion. A couple of yards behind it were five kites, motionless, respectfully waiting, in the humblest posture, for some leavings. They seemed very small beside the vulture, which is certainly the biggest bird on the wing I have seen so far. I was able to get within some forty yards of it, and I noticed particularly its light head. The rest of the body was dark, save for a stripe on the wings, visible when it was in flight. I shall find out its name from Iñes Bey, who has already identified the black and white birds I saw in the Mokattam hills. They are the *Saxicola lugens* and the *Saxicola albipygaca*. As the names were given me on the strength of my description, I shall not be certain until I have seen the stuffed specimens. The day I saw the vulture I also saw a kind of fox or jackal which suddenly appeared on a ridge near us, then hurriedly took off. It had the gait of a wolf, but its tail was very bushy, and I do not sufficiently recall what a jackal looks like to be sure about it. I also thought that it was longer and taller than a fox, but you would not believe what strange mistakes one makes in the desert about the proportions of things for lack of a basis of comparison.

I have come across a spot often visited by tourists on donkey-back, the "Well of Moses." It is a small brackish pool lying in a rock hollow on the floor of a basin to the east of the Mokattam hills. It would be attractive were it not for shards of champagne bottles and the droppings of the sheep and goats which come there to drink. The penetrating odor arising from all this reminded me of a sheepfold behind Plumat.

Last Sunday, there was a big procession at Matariya[1] in honor of the Immaculate Conception; I took a fairly active

---

[1] A small place east of Cairo, not far from the obelisk of Heliopolis. Tradition has it that this was where the Holy Family stayed after their flight from Judea. A church was built at Matariya in 1903–1904.

part in it, of course, on account of my altar boys. The ceremony really went off very well. In addition to the school, there was a crowd of guests, and all the best Catholic society of Cairo. There were even a hundred-odd Irish soldiers in uniform who sang some very lovely English hymns.

The day before yesterday, we had the first real rainfall since my arrival; it did not last long, but immediately afterward we were wading in mud. Since it became almost impossible to conduct classes, the boys were sent home two hours earlier; this is what usually happens, apparently, with the result that they are delighted when the first drops fall.

Goodbye, dear Father and Mother. Again, a happy new year to you all. I kiss you. Thank Toto for his letter.

Pierre

Could you send me Guiguite's address, and also Françoise's, which I have lost.

A happy new year to all again. Did you finally receive my letter of the beginning of December, as well as the one of the 16th?

Yesterday I found some big scorpions!

I kiss you and don't forget you.

Pierre

10a

Cairo, December 17, 1905

Dear Father,

In addition to the enclosed letter with news of the fortnight, I have to write to you more especially for Christmas. Even though only three of your children will be there to wish you a happy Christmas on the 24th, you know that all of them, particularly those in heaven, at Tourcoing and here, will pray for you and will say "Happy Christmas" to you in thought even more affectionately than in the past. I wanted to say this as in previous years. I shall ask for you whatever you want most dearly, particularly that your children may always remain good and become men. Thank you again for everything you have done for me, you and Mother, and remember that I love you very much, as ever.

Pierre

11

Cairo, January 4, 1906

Dear Father and Mother,

You must have received my new year's wishes just after Christmas, followed, I hope, by some photographs of the cultivated areas around Cairo. Since the desert has few admirers, I could not find any views of it. I hope that will come. So I will only repeat to you what I said before: I wish you, all of you, a happy new year, such as our Lord desires for the family. Guiguite has written to me from Cannes, where she seems to be making the best of things very bravely, and is happy to be able to teach little girls their catechism. From what Mother wrote me, I expect you have kept that lucky fellow, Joseph; but owing to the postal delays at the new year I have not yet received any direct news from you.

Right now I am on vacation, and a very busy one too, on account of the arrival here of some young teachers from Alexandria, friends from Jersey and Aix; they will be here for these few days. To people coming from Alexandria, Cairo is—quite understandably—an enchanted city, and we who are privileged to see its marvels daily are only too happy to show them to others. For the past three days, I have been showing Guy Le Marois around; he is thrilled at the sight of the powerful automobiles which line the great avenues of Cairo in the absence of the roads of Egypt, which are still to be constructed. By the way, his brother, the sailor, will probably leave for Saigon at the end of January.[1] I immediately thought of Uncle Georges, who will receive him rather as he used to receive Albéric.[2] Last Sunday I thought of Albéric a lot; it was at Ismailia, looking out over the thin little ribbon of Suez. I thought that he must certainly have seen the dunes where I was standing, and I was quite moved, though not in any melancholy fashion.

This brings me to tell you about Ismailia, where I accompanied a little French boy whose father is an agent of the Suez Canal Company. It is a pleasant three-hour trip from here, by express train, and the journey is agreeable, especially after the cotton town of Zagazig where the Delta—which is monotonous at this time with its clover fields—gives place to the desert. In addition to my pupil, I had to take charge of two little French girls, his friends, as big as Loulou would be now, or a little younger, whose fathers also work for the Suez Canal Company. These interesting little girls did not make a nuisance of themselves, and amused me with their conversation, which reminded me of everything Mother or others had told me about the Sacred Heart. For they are at the Sacred Heart school here. A big boarding school is under construction; I don't despair of seeing Aunt Louise there. One of them had the "ribbon"!

I spent six hours at Ismailia. The town is not interesting, but the location is lovely; right in the yellow desert, with its bare mountains on the horizon, and at the edge of a dark blue lagoon traversed by the Canal. The town is bordered by large and beautiful parks, with palm trees and woods of a kind of big conifer (primitive) (of Oceania, *Casuarina* . . .) which is

[1] He has just exchanged posts. [Note by Father Teilhard de Chardin.]
[2] Pierre's older brother, the second in the family (the first, Marielle, died in infancy). He was a naval officer and died in 1902.

more like shave-grass than pine. You can walk along immense avenues, shaded by tall lebbek acacias, without meeting a single stroller. One of them leads to the place where the Canal joins the lagoon. I was able to take a long look at it, from the hut of a friendly guard where I was taking shelter from a sudden storm. Nothing passed except dredgers or tugs. Since the next day was January 1, business was probably slow. At the water's edge were masses of little dead seahorses, beautiful shells bristling with spikes, jellyfish, cuttlefish, small fish resembling chub. The desert there is much sandier than near Cairo. When I left in the evening, I saw a band of Russians passing, emigrating; they looked extraordinary, booted and wearing rabbitskin caps. Some, wearing pointed turbans, looked like Tartars. I do not know where they were bound.

Yesterday, a number of us went to Saqqara, on the left bank of the Nile, south of Cairo; I believe I indicated it on the little map I sent you in September. We set off by train at 7, and two stops from Cairo found a number of donkeys waiting to take us to the Pyramids. For three or four miles we traveled through the cultivated green band which constitutes inhabited Egypt. This part is astonishingly beautiful, with its palm trees, green fields, big sheets of water with mud villages alongside them, the whole enclosed between two yellow bands of desert, very rocky to the east, sandier to the west, where we were headed. It is in this flat and muddy band that the ruins of Memphis are buried, an immense city whose finest stones the Arabs carried off to build Cairo. Two gigantic statues of Ramses repose under the palms, one of granite, the other of limestone; the head, which I would prosaically compare in size to a large barrel, has a singularly fine expression, smiling, like all Egyptian statues. Here and there, amid the earth shanties, one finds great blocks of Seyenetic rose granite from Aswan which might just as well have been brought from Corbières to Jersey.

The donkey cavalcade was great fun, and in the morning no one was pitched over the head of his mount. Before 10 we were ascending the first slopes of the desert, which are completely ploughed up by excavations. There is a group of Pyramids here, relatively small and fairly dilapidated; and from a distance one can see the Giza Pyramids. The Dacrur ones are quite far away. One of them has the corners cut off, indicating that the architects must have abandoned an over-ambitious initial plan. Among those we visited the best preserved, unique of its kind, and oldest of all, is in tiers formed not of massive slabs, but of stones more or less cemented together. Here art was still in its infancy.

By far the most curious part of our visit was to the cities of the dead built underground in the middle of the desert, around the Pyramids. Four or five tombs have been unearthed there, each comprising a series of chambers adorned with marvelous hieroglyphics, often painted blue, and very well preserved. This was the soul house of the deceased, closed by a fictitious door, a kind of stele through which the soul was believed to go in and out of the other world. On it are represented all the good things the deceased enjoyed in his lifetime. There are scenes of hippopotamus hunting, of fishing. The movement of the animals and fish is very well caught; there is less delicacy than in Japanese etchings, and in any case this is sculpture, but I could easily recognize a number of fish which I had seen in the Nile aquarium. For instance, there is a hippopotamus pinning a struggling crocodile with its jaws; the victim's plight is less fortunate. Still underground, and hewn right in the rock face—which is very soft, by the way—is the famous Serapeum with the tombs of the Apis bulls. Each tomb (there are about twenty of them) is in a rectangular chamber opening onto the main passage, which is a good 650 yards long. The most remarkable thing is the tomb itself, an immense slab (about 4 x 4 x 7 yards), usually of polished rose granite, with hieroglyphics engraved upon it. One wonders how anyone managed to drag such slabs through an underground trench and set them in position. One tomb is unfinished; the unpolished slab was abandoned in the middle of a passage.

We had dinner in a kind of barracks known as the hermitage of Mariette, who stayed there when he was conducting his excavations. After which we visited another interior of a Pyramid, which is itself partially in ruins, but with a tomb in a marvelous state of preservation. It is reached by a ramp leading to chambers with pointed ceilings entirely covered with inscriptions. Close by is a (modern) spiral stairway, descending some forty yards to a tomb. Toward the end of our visit, the wind rose, and as we left, whirling clouds of sand were rising from the desert, providing real "local color." It cannot be easy to get around in such weather. Our return trip was punctuated by some hilarious spills which I was spared.

In the fields there were quite a lot of plovers and a flock of red-breasted swallows. They cannot have found Egypt particularly hospitable of late. Unheard-of event in at least twenty-five years—one night the temperature was 27 degrees! The results were disastrous in some parts for the banana trees, rubber trees, etc. The garden at Matariya, with its many exotic trees, took a particularly bad beating. Now the temperature has returned to normal. Apparently around Beirut, at an altitude of 1200 yards, the temperature was 13° below, which I find rather astonishing; but the report comes from the place itself. The students were amazed to see a little ice.

I have just received all your letters. I intend to read the article Father refers to on eolithic flints. It seems that in some parts of Egypt, such as Thebes, there are many cut stones to be found.

My congratulations to Joseph; I hope he will manage to use his freedom to work intelligently.

Mother will be pleased to know that at Matariya I saw the

vestments made of Albéric's Chinese silk, which I easily recognized; there is also an altar cloth of blue silk of the same provenance, if I am not mistaken.

Goodbye, dear Father and Mother, I kiss you, as well as Joseph and Toto, and I pray for you. Since this letter will of course go on to Cannes, I want Guiguite to know that I shall try to write to her before too long.

Your child,

Pierre

12

Cairo, January 22, 1906

Dear Father and Mother,

This time again I am very late in writing to you; the opening of the new term is the reason; for in addition to the usual difficulty of getting into harness again after a vacation, I had to handle a part of the program which took quite some time, such as preparing courses and experiments. But it seems to me that the hardest part of the year, and perhaps of my teaching career, is over. In a month I shall begin reviewing with the philosophers, candidates in May, and since I do not do much more than repeat what I said before in the other classes, with a few adaptations, you can see that the bulk of the work has been done. There remain the critical moments of the examination to which our students attach an almost fetishistic importance; —for which you cannot really blame them, since the Egyptian baccalaureate is a passport to jobs in most areas. The great advantage of my present position is that I know my boys. Naturally I have most contact with the "science" sections, and a good many among them are eager to learn, so that it is a pleasure to open up horizons for them. I have my classes with them in the evening. In the morning I have to cope with the somewhat restive crowd of humanists, those in third especially, whom one is reduced to threatening with detentions and bad marks. But there are no "rumpuses" such as one gets in our schools in France. With Thursdays and Sundays off, I still have time to work, and the days pass quickly; one wishes they were longer, for there is nothing like teaching to give one a thirst for study.

A fortnight ago I made use of my knowledge of the topography of the desert to take a group of older boys out there—for longer, perhaps, than they would have wished. Most of them are lamentably lazy. I tried, not altogether unsuccessfully, to awaken in some of them a first taste for natural history at the sight of an oyster bed and cirithiod fossils. One of them assured me that there were still quite a few hyenas to be found only a mile or so from here.

On the subject of zoology, I have seen Iñes Bey again, and he is more and more affable. He let me take a glimpse at some specimens of Egyptian fauna other than those he had had at his place on my first visit; I shall try to see them in more detail. I was surprised to learn that the Nile still harbors fine turtles, and that a host of strange animals are to be found in the Cairo vicinity: jerboas, thorny rats, a kind of pretty skunk with black and white stripes, big lizards with spiky tails (*uromastyx*), not to speak of magnificent two-horned vipers, cobras and even (after the name of its "inventor"), *Walterinesia,* a poisonous snake which is completely black and a good size. It seems that the baboons and dog-faced baboons which Arabs often have on leashes here come from the Red Sea coast (Suakin), where they live in the desert rocks.

The day after I wrote you last, I made my longest trip this year. My friend Bovier and I set out for a whole day in the desert, and in all that time the only living things we saw were some grasshoppers and five or six camels, all alone, at the bottom of a wadi. On the other hand, we collected some lovely shells and coral fossil, and enjoyed some magnificent views. We had set out in a southeasterly direction, where the terrain is increasingly mountainous. It is not yet too high there, but very rocky and broken up. These parts are marked "gypaetus" on the map; and from a distance I saw a large bird of prey. They must be vultures; I saw five or six specimens again on carrion near Cairo.

On the last day of the vacation, I went with my friends from Alexandria to the dam which was constructed long ago to the north, approximately where the waters of the Nile divide. This dam is interesting chiefly because of the very beautiful botanical gardens cultivated on an island, in a marvelous location. There is a pool full of lotuses, which I should dearly love to see in flower. That is where I saw the finest papyri, taller than I am, with big flowers in silky tufts. You know that the only place papyrus still grows wild is in the Sudan, whence perhaps the Egyptians used to import it. I saw my second "pharaoh's rat" in the pool I mentioned just now. I met some wild-fowl hunters; notwithstanding their Nimrod-like air, they had bagged little more sensational than a young flamingo.

A more archeological operation: we proceeded to explore the "rubbish mounds," massive hills bordering the city to the north and south, and entirely composed of debris accumulated through the centuries. You find regular layers composed of scoriae and potsherds of all kinds, going back to Roman times.

It has been possible to reconstruct the history of Arab pottery by means of all these fragments. Our loot for the moment amounts to three or four Coptic or Arab medals which we shall show Iñes, and a few fine pieces of stoneware marked with the armorial bearings of sultans of Mamelukes. These large vacant terrains are very curious, and the view there is very unusual, given the purely Arab character of the neighboring sections. Somewhere under the rubbish mounds to the south are the ruins of the city of Fostat, which its inhabitants burned down rather than let it fall into the hands of the crusaders.

Yesterday, the school's feast day, we had a solemn Mass in the Chaldean rite. Some of the ceremonies are truly beautiful, but we are not attuned to the monotonous and shapeless chants which continue right through the ceremony. Yesterday's Mass took only three-quarters of an hour, but we were told, not without a touch of pride, that it might have continued for three hours.

The climax of the school feast day is always the big Arab play, which will be performed on Friday (a Moslem holiday) before a select audience of Arabs of consequence. I am curious to see what it will be like. Let us hope that there will be no hitch as at Alexandria; the Arab play of December 3 coincided with the small uprising, which sadly depleted the audience.

Between my last letter and this one, we had a renewal of vows here. The preparatory triduum is not, of course, what it is in the atmosphere of recollection of the scholasticate, but this is inevitable in our job, and it is still for our Lord.

Here, Father Garraud periodically and anxiously inquires about the fate of the Bansac house, and I can only answer with shamefaced silence. He assures me that he has heard sinister rumors on the subject.

I have received all your letters regularly.

Now you are at Clermont again; do you know that the school bell, the only one, incidentally, that I hear in this place, reminds me of the bells of the Carmelites on Saturday evenings?

I enclose a photo of Cairo seen from the school terrace. It is the east. On the horizon is Mokattam, bounded to the right by the Citadel and its lovely mosque, something like Santa Sophia. To be noted, with a magnifying glass, are the innumerable minarets; two-thirds of them are along a single street; these are very Arab sections. The grey slopes against which they stand out (?) below the white cliffs of Mokattam are the rubbish mounds. The European part of Cairo would follow to the right of the photo.

Goodbye, dear Father and Mother, I kiss you, as well as Joseph

67

and Toto, and I pray hard for you. I have received a nice letter from Françoise. Tell Guiguite that I have received all of hers. I kiss her too.

Pierre

13

Cairo, February 10, 1906

Dear Father and Mother,

For a wonder, it is raining this evening, to the dismay of the Dominican Father who is giving a series of lectures in our auditorium (if Françoise could hear me!), and to the delight of the students, who expect—but vainly—to go home early. I have told you before that Cairo becomes demoralized when it rains; all the tarbooshes are covered with handkerchiefs, and I have just seen a coachman unashamedly holding up an umbrella as he drives his buggy. This weather comes after a day of hot wind, preluding the famous khamsins of April and May which put the tourists to flight. I think the cold weather is really over, though it may still be cool.

Since my last letter, all of yours have reached me very regularly, particularly Mother's "galleons." I am sending her a reply herewith.

The big event here was the Arab play, which went off very well indeed. In accordance with Arab custom, the audience was exclusively male, and impressive as well as spectacular—all in tarbooshes or turbans. In the first row sat two ministers and the governor of Cairo, with a great array of pashas.

Other than the emotions that might be aroused by an adaptation of *For the Crown*, the chief interest of the play was its language. You know that literary Arabic (vocabulary, and especially syntax) is a language closed to the mass of the people, which erudite sheiks learn as Chinese mandarins learn characters. Consequently, what this gathering appreciated, not without a touch of national pride, was the choice of words and the strict grammatical sequences, as much as, if not even more than the ideas.

Personally, as a nonexpert, responsible for lighting behind the scenes, I found that Orientals recite remarkably well, and this, incidentally, is the unanimous opinion. The actors, moreover, all students or former students, were garbed in the rich costumes of Bedouins.

Last Sunday was one of their big holidays; the streets were filled with little boys, and particularly with little girls, in red, light green or even golden dresses, all blowing hewgags for all they were worth. That is clearly the most popular toy.

You must certainly have read in the papers about the launching of the Berber-Suakin railroad which is to serve the British Sudan by way of the Red Sea independently of Egypt. Everyone sees in this the obvious intention of the British to shut themselves up in their own preserves. For the same reason they are not completing a section of the line which would link Aswan to Khartoum.

With the heat, the animals are beginning to emerge, and in the desert one can see lizards and agamas scurrying about again. I have also seen three foxes in succession in the desert; the burrows were plainly visible, and obviously inhabited.

Cairo definitely advances every day. The buses drawn by thin and stubborn mules which transported the natives are beginning to give way to large automobiles which unfortunately give off an excess of fumes. What was most strange was the enthusiasm of the Arabs, who besieged the cars during the first few days.

Periodically, these days, students bring me the presents they received last month to make them work—many of them were "electricity boxes," with batteries, a little motor, a spool, etc. If

Uncle Louis du R. still had to buy interesting Christmas gifts, these would be just the right thing. I don't imagine that Toto would ever want one. Has Collot been found?

Goodbye, dear Father and Mother, I kiss you as well as Joseph and Toto, and I pray for you.

Pierre

I noted that there had been fighting at the Versailles church.[1] Could Uncle René have been there by any chance? Or rather, is it possible that he was not there?

[1] This was the time of the "inventories" in France.

71

14

Cairo, March 1, 1906

Dear Father and Mother,

So here we are, with the carnival behind us. It was conducted with much the same rituals as at Mongré—a lottery and various sideshows—except that on Shrove Tuesday all the boys were sent off to their relatives or friends.

The students have no reason to complain this year. A famous quartet of Austrian violinists (one of the successes of the Cairo season) came to give a recital gratis, and the music was very beautiful. The same day an actor of the Chat Noir (who happens to be the nephew of a former music instructor at Mongré, whom I knew well) showed the "Sphinx" with slides. At any rate, that had local interest.

Cairo, as you see, has plenty to offer: motor buses are becoming increasingly numerous, and tomorrow a part of the school is going to view a moving picture, the very best, apparently. Despite these advances in civilization, I had my first camel ride the day before yesterday. My friend Bovier-Lap. and I wanted to reach a fossil bed located quite far from the Pyramids, in the Libyan desert, so we hired a desert-ship for the day, and this provided us with plenty of impressions of wild and nomadic life. The seasickness which one is purported to feel on these animals is a myth, and their slow and rhythmical gait is very restful; like all of its kind, the camel which carried us religiously grumbled or snorted at each additional effort. We won it over by bringing it the occasional green plants which we found in our path, and then by stuffing it with orange peel, crusts of bread and cheese, etc. It had a priceless expression, with its pendulous lips and big shining eyes. To find oneself in the middle of the desert on this mount was no less characteristic of the Egyptian scene. The camel rendered us considerable services, incidentally, not only in carrying our fossils back, but in getting about in a region which is very sandy and where walking quickly becomes difficult.

This excursion opened up new horizons for me to the north-west, in the direction of the Natrun valley. These horizons, incidentally, are nothing more than sand dunes as far as the eye can see. Apparently the Natrun valley itself, with its lakes and deep depressions, is a very curious territory. I did not see a single animal, apart from a small predatory bird, but many tracks of foxes or jackals and of rats. This is the area where one most frequently finds the kind of skunk with white stripes which I saw stuffed at Iñes Bey's. But these are all hidden by day. It was not too hot, by the way, though the temperature is beginning to rise substantially.

Imagine, right now all the state schools, higher and secondary, are on strike. Young people hold meetings, make emotional speeches, and the newspapers acclaim this unexpected awakening from Egyptian torpor. It will be interesting to see how the Minister of Public Education handles the problem. For a while his own son was delegated by his friends to present grievances! Meanwhile, the law schools, medical schools, agricultural schools, etc. are deserted. The most interesting part of it all is that the government has made it clear in the past few years that it was in urgent need of young people to fill the various posts.

I have received all your letters. Our good Gonzague is certainly proving himself indomitable, and Yer-Yer must appreciate him as a brother worthy of respect. I hope, however, that he will calm down; I shall try to drop him a line.

The boys in my class are beginning to worry about the examinations, which take place in two months. Lent will be a time of cramming, harder for the students than for the teacher, who does not have anything new to teach. However, I have not altogether completed my course as yet; I shall probably have done so by the time I write again.

I read about the verdict against Uncle Alphonse in the papers. All these affairs, plus those concerning Germany, must make the atmosphere quite gloomy in France. But I have been abroad so long that I do not really know what the reaction is likely to be.

Goodbye, dear Father and Mother. I kiss you as well as Joseph and Toto, and pray hard for you. I should like to write to Guiguite before the end of the week. I don't know whether I shall be able to.

Pierre

P.S. We have the Shelley book here. My thanks to Father.

15

Cairo, March 19, 1906

Dear Father and Mother,

As I begin this letter, I recall that, seven years ago, my departure for Aix was only a few hours away, and I should find it quite difficult to disentangle all the sentiments which that memory evokes. I think it can all be summed up, really, in a great deal of affection for you, and of gratitude to our Lord. You know how much I always pray to him for you and love you from the bottom of my heart. I tell myself that at this same moment Françoise, surrounded by the elite (?) of Tourcoing, is presiding over the banquet for the aged.[1] In Cairo, too, there are old people, but they are not cared for by the Little Sisters, which is not at all the same. Some of the inmates, at least, are very colorful, among them an old Negress who is a dance-band enthusiast; every time she hears an instrument being tuned she claps her hands and utters piercing shrieks, and is surprised and annoyed because "it does not go on."

My most important news about the past fortnight is that I have finally finished my course with the philosophers; "review" is in full swing, and I realized the other day that I had only

[1] Banquet on the feast of St. Joseph, a great feast day for the Little Sisters of the Poor.

thirty-odd classes to give them. Let us hope that the examination of May 7 will be auspicious for them!

In connection with study, the rebels of the Cairo University, after holding turbulent meetings—I could see the swarm of tarbooshes from a distance—and swearing on the Bible and the Koran, suddenly bowed before a very chilly circular from Lord Cromer. Order has been completely restored; a happy aftermath is that certain privileges have been granted to this year's candidates for the Egyptian baccalaureate.

I have been scouring Mokattam for fossils, with tolerable success. The correspondent of the Museum here, worthy Mr. Fourtan, classifies my fossils for me. He showed me a completely new type of sea-urchin which he had just found, and I was able, a week later, to bring him another specimen. Meanwhile I was struck by the abundance of swifts in the rocks of the said Mokattam. I had not heard them (of course) since Montorgueil and Sarcenat, and it is a curious sensation to hear them in late February and March. They are accompanied by an ash-grey rock swallow, which is very tame.

It must be admitted that, apart from a brief renewal of a cool spell since yesterday, we are coming to the first forewarnings of the hot season. Now it is the turn of a kind of creeper known as Bougainvillea to flower; it grows in all the gardens, on the walls and arbors; it is a marvelous purple color.

I want to thank Father for his information about the clumps of shrubs in the plains.

As regards Abbé Le Dantec, I had indeed heard of him. As far as I can judge, he is right in many respects concerning "aviation," where experimental data are insufficient, so that mathematicians have often been in error. But I greatly fear that without those same mathematicians he would not have been able to arrive at his laws, "so beautiful and so simple," which presuppose considerable work by mathematicians.

Last Thursday an automobile garage burnt down here, lock,

stock and barrel, to the elation of the boys, who never stopped talking about it the following day. Apparently the fire brigade took a half-hour to arrive at the scene, although the fire station is only ten minutes' walk away. The equipment is excellent, but the personnel is inadequate.

You can imagine how closely we follow French affairs here. The "Ponaux" are fine folk; is there supposed to be anything remotely like them in the mountains?

The school has finally been to the cinema, which is the big hit in Cairo. Since the management of the cinema is entirely in the hands of former students, you will not be surprised to hear that the entire school was invited. Incidentally, this was their best publicity, for from the very next Sunday on, three-quarters of the parents cannot have enjoyed any peace until they took their precious children back there. It was an impressive demonstration; at least three hundred students filing through the streets of Cairo in a steady stream. Such a thing was unprecedented, and the rubbernecks thought it was a new phase in the school strike, which was then at its height. To come back to the cinema, it has passed the stage of the familiar or merely exotic scenes which we used to see at Lumière. These are large-scale fake sets: stories of Indians, trips to the moon, etc.; the whole very well done, by the way.

I was agreeably surprised to hear that Biel was having such a long vacation. It is nice of him to work as he does, and a salutary example to the younger ones.

Goodbye, dear Father and Mother, I kiss you, as well as Toto and Joseph.

Your child,

Pierre

P.S. I did not know that Galliéni was at Clermont. I heard a lot about him from the Madagascar fathers, who were not enthusiastic about him at all.

A good old Brother, named Ricolène, a native of Ceyrat, has just died. He used to talk to me endlessly about Auvergne.

16

Cairo, April 8, 1906

Dear Father and Mother,

I hasten to take advantage of my first free moment to write
to you, for these days we are quite busy. The reason is the
examinations: preliminary tests for the upper classes, Easter
examinations for the lower ones, and then one has to correct
or lay down the law as the case may be. This morning I had to
give the fourth their catechism examinations, which was a lot
of fun for me, probably because this was the first time I had
been dealing with younger boys, and there was a minimum of
disciplinary problems. More prolonged contact with them would
probably have speedily disenchanted me somewhat.

And now Holy Week is approaching, with its ceremonies,
rather frightening for one responsible for altar boys who is so
little of a liturgist as I. But after that will come the vacation;
I shall not be completely free, since the May candidates will
be coming in from time to time for review, but that is nothing
very onerous.

I hope you will have pleasant weather during Easter week.
Your cold weather has found some echo here, in the sense that
up until today the atmosphere has been notably fresher. I am
comparing it with last week, when we had the first little khamsin.
That is the term used for the desert wind which blows espe-

cially in spring, in theory for forty days. Really hot gusts of wind arrive, as hot as in front of an oven, and the sky becomes grey with dust. I went up to the terrace to see how Cairo looked in this state: for half an hour one could hardly distinguish anything further off than 500 to 1000 yards. Everything was shrouded in a cloud of dust. The Prince of Wales arrived at that point, but preceded by a rainfall which washed everything clean and enabled me to enjoy, in the desert, the sensation of an autumn hunt in a volcanic outflow of Auvergne, with fine rain and overhanging clouds.

I did not see the Prince of Wales, only the very numerous flags hung out in his honor, and some of the noble sheiks invited to an equestrian performance passing gravely on their little horses or white dromedaries. Apparently the popular reception was somewhat chilly, and the British soldiers were jeered at. But I would not dare vouch for this. It is a fact that the Arab papers increasingly accuse England of using all Egypt's finances to colonize the Sudan; but the Arab readers around here seem to me too apathetic to concern themselves with grievances which actually affect them rather indirectly.

In any case, they have been too busy these days welcoming the pilgrims from Mecca, back with the sacred carpet, to bother about the Prince of Wales. Each pilgrim is regarded as something of a saint, worthy from now on to wear the green turban. As soon as he arrives at the station, a whole retinue awaiting in the neighboring cafés places itself at his disposal. The procession is headed by two camels, ridiculously bedecked with red and gold velvet, bells, mirrors, etc., and mounted by little Arabs playing kettledrums for all they are worth. Behind them come dancers, gesticulating as they perform their war dances with swords and microscopic shields. Then come the masked men, carrying sticks with small grills attached; these grills are filled with inflammable material at night and covered with red cloth by day. Finally the hero appears, often riding in a cab (!), and in full

Arab regalia. I have even seen a big seventeenth century carriage exhibited, entirely gilded, with footmen in the rear, all wearing French costumes. This odd vehicle is brought out from time to time for important weddings; it is doubtless some custom dating back about 300 years. But what do you think of a country which crystallizes customs we have already forgotten, and at the same time retains agricultural methods which have not changed by one jot since the days of the Pharaohs?

I was thinking about that the other day as I was walking in the rich fields alongside the Nile, covered with a thick harvest of short-eared and long-bearded wheat. For I did finally get to the Nile banks, mainly in order to collect samples for a conchologist of Oran (Mr. Pallary), who had written to me asking for shells from Egypt. The most remarkable are the unadorned type of desert helix, the kind one is amazed to see moving across the showcases in the British Museum more than a year after they have been labeled. But the Nile can be interesting. The first time, I saw only unios (three species at most). One of the specimens, instead of being just pearly, is a beautiful deep purple. My grievance against the Nile, at least the Nile in Lower Egypt, is that it is so muddy, and offers nothing but ooze at its edges. But otherwise its banks are very gay and restful due to the richness of their vegetation (agricultural), though a little too crowded with sakiehs (chain pumps) turned by small, blindfolded bulls. I saw some fine specimens of gamoosas. Despite their resemblance to the hippopotamus, they apparently produce a lot of milk. If Vialles were warmer, one could adapt them there.

I was forgetting to tell you that some 6 miles from here, in the desert, I found a big basalt bed which the geologists either had never discovered or had forgotten. There are sheets of basalt almost everywhere between here and Sinai, and their black hue adds a final touch of gloom to the desert. I enjoyed

81

being on volcanic terrain, not to speak of the new possibilities opened to me in minerology.

I have received all your letters, and also one from Biel in answer to mine. I was impressed, but not surprised, at his offhand references to the authorities who teach him.

Goodbye, dear Father and Mother. I kiss you as well as those whom the vacation will have brought to you by the time this letter arrives. You know how much I think of you and pray for you.

Pierre

17

Cairo, April 24, 1906

Dear Father and Mother,

Although it is now 5:30 p.m., the thermometer as I write to you stands at nearly 91 degrees, and at noon it read over 97 degrees in the shade. This constitutes the first serious onslaught of the khamsin, and it does not bother me at all, except of course in that the desert is inaccessible in such weather. There it must have been at least 104 degrees all day. It seems that the longer one lives in Egypt, the more sensitive one becomes to the heat; it is a fact that this morning my May candidates were pretty demoralized.

Now for the news of the last two weeks. First, you have learned from the papers of the death of Father Martin;[1] this is a great loss to the Society, for all who saw him were agreed about the unusual elevation and breadth of his views. He was one of those to whom we may be sure God will send worthy successors. I had also learned, shortly before your letters arrived, of the death of Father Rochette.[2] These were beautiful deaths.

As anticipated, Holy Week for me was abundantly filled

1 A Spaniard, superior general of the Society of Jesus.
2 Father Henri Rochette de Lempdes (1834–1906) was related to the Teilhards; he was endowed with an iron will, and was a forceful rector of schools (Mongré, Moulins, Marseilles, Lyons) until the law of 1901.

with ceremonies and examinations. The latter continued not to worry me, and the former were satisfactory. If I am left in tenure, I shall know my way about next year. The hardest thing, really, is to keep the youngsters more or less quiet on Holy Saturday for an hour before they go on vacation.

On Holy Thursday I made some rather unusual visits to altars of repose; it was almost like making voyages of exploration. There is an old section here with tortuous and unbelievably narrow streets, where chapels of every conceivable rite are tucked away—Coptic, Maronite, Armenian, Greek, etc., relics of the days when Catholics were confined to a sort of ghetto in the midst of Moslem Cairo. Thanks to two good ladies who were also making the rounds, and in whose steps we followed, we were able to find all these churches, most of which are unrecognizable from the outside.

As I told you, my older students continued to come last week. That did not prevent me from making a day-long excursion on Easter Monday in the mountains between Cairo and Helwan (some 17 miles to the south, on the right bank of the Nile). We spent the morning visiting the ancient Egyptian quarries cut right into the cliff which bounds the mountains where they reach the Nile plain. Arabs today fear the holes and work only in the open. Their predecessors, wishing to follow the beds of good rock, managed to dig very large, beautiful galleries which reminded me of those I saw at St. Paul Trois Châteaux during my pilgrimage in the novitiate. Here and there the workers had carved a stele, or some religious scene, or crudely painted pharaonic tablets. We even found a very well preserved Greek inscription addressed to an Alexander II and his family. What was very beautiful was to see the Nile valley from the desert through the wide bay openings, with on the further bank a series of fifteen to twenty Pyramids or fragments of Pyramids. These quarries produced the stone used in the construction of the Pyramids, and there are still traces of the causeway over which the stone was hauled. The distance is very considerable, and there was the Nile to cross.

In the evening, we left the Nile valley to penetrate a little further east. It was a good thing we did, for there are real little mountains here (485 yards high, but they begin at a level of at most 40 yards), very bare, but jagged and broken by precipices, from which one looks down on heights of at least 130 yards. It is all completely wild, and the horizon is immense. I found quite a number of fossils, oysters especially; but I also brought back a nice nautilus, as well as some present-day helixes for my correspondent from Oran. There were a few pretty flowers in the wadi beds, among others a little garnet-red figwort; but my friend Bovier, lacking [familiarity with] Egyptian flora and [the assistance of] native botanists, is rather at a loss in classifying the flora of the wadis. That day (Easter Monday) was a local holiday, Sham-el-Nessim, when everyone in Cairo, complete with family and a cold picnic dinner, hops on the suburban trains for a picnic in the country. Since the country to which they repair is not, of course, the desert, we were as usual alone, except that on our way back the Cairo trains were crowded to the point of causing us serious delay.

On Thursday of Easter Week, the whole staff of the school traveled on a small steamboat to the dam constructed at the point where the Nile forks in two (the Rosetta and Damietta branches). The main attraction of the dam is a beautiful park maintained by the state. I had seen it in January; now it has a fairylike aspect, being filled with exotic flowers and trees whose names, unfortunately, the administration neglects to indicate. There is a profusion, especially, of great aloes, with flowers several yards high, and a whole population of lizards, among them many uromastix; they are fat, with the head of a chameleon and a tail bristling with spikes, and they are good tree-climbers. In the sands of the Nile I found clouds of small tiger-beetles, of a type unfamiliar to me, and I had a terrible time collecting only five or six specimens. I don't think I have ever seen coleoptera which fly so well; these indulge in the luxury of circling before they settle, like flies.

The trip down the Nile allowed me to see great flocks of ducks at fairly close range; they were quite small, with dark tails, and a stripe on the white wings. There were literally swarms of small grey swallows, their nests dug in the mud of the bank. While I am on the subject of fauna, it will interest Guiguite to know the approximate description of two kinds of carabids which my friend Bovier-Lapierre brought back from Ismailia, where he had gone in his turn to escort some students. Unlike me, he did not find a shore covered with small sea-horses, but instead, insects had made their appearance. The figured carabids are absolutely black, with spots of dull white which look as if they had been applied with thick oil paint. I believe the species is fairly common in Africa. Last winter, Iñes Bey told me about a married couple, both of them naturalists, who had just passed through Cairo on their way to Kharthoum to find carabids of this or similar types. No. 2, very different from its neighbor, made a strident noise as soon as they tried to catch it. Ismailia also yielded an enormous scarite, but of the altogether conventional type.

Last Sunday, in torrid heat, I came across a huge spider, as long as eleven or twelves of the squares of the paper on which I am writing, and covered with long golden hairs. It must have been suddenly disturbed, and was obviously trying to hide in the shadow of our feet. Unfortunately I had no jar to put it in; while I was trying to hold it in place with my hammer to observe it better, an Arab expressed profound terror of it and urged us to kill it. It must be a poisonous kind; but according to Iñes Bey, there is none in Egypt whose sting is normally fatal.

I am continuing my letter Wednesday morning (25th); school has just reopened in a temperature which seems likely to top yesterday's, to the greater joy of the vegetation. The lebbek acacias, the principal source of shade here, are shedding the last of their leaves, which presages the early burgeoning of new ones. Some are already turning green. The barbary fig trees are clothing themselves in big yellow flowers, and butterflies are appearing—the Danais type, or just common cabbage butterflies. I did not tell you that for nearly two months now we have been having strawberries; the figs and apricots (called mishmish) are quite large.

During the vacation, some of the students, with Reverend Father Rector, made the pilgrimage to Jerusalem, together with a group from Alexandria. It is becoming an established custom. They are coming back today, and it cannot be very cool for them in the train, especially between Port Said and Ismailia.

Last evening I received Father's letter of the 17th. I cannot enlighten him as to the exact source of the desert basalt; Sinai is granitic, but the mountains of the Red Sea are sufficiently volcanic to be regarded as a possible source.

Goodbye, dear Father and Mother, I kiss you as well as Guiguite, Joseph, Toto. You know how much I love and pray for you.

Pierre

18

Dear Father and Mother,

Today the candidates for the Egyptian baccalaureate are writing their final essays, and it is physics day for the students in the humanities section. However, this subject carries so few credits for them that I am very little concerned about it. The science students, for whom it is really important, did their written examination on Tuesday and are satisfied. Personally I am sorry that they should have been given such easy questions. My students were good, and a less banal subject would probably have made them excel, which is useful when the examinees are legion, as they are this year—nearly 800 of them. A huge tent had to be set up to hold them. Another disadvantage of such numbers is that the results will not be known for at least three weeks. This was obviously the major event of the fortnight.

Preparations are actively going forward in the school for a performance of *Voyage to China* in honor of Father Rector's birthday, on Sunday the 20th. It promises to go well, and the star feature is to be a set representing a ship's bridge, with masts, funnel and seascape.

I am of course very relieved at the departure of the philosophy students, and my year is virtually completed. Many of the boys are thinking along the same lines, and are beginning to talk of leaving shortly for Europe, and especially for France, where any more or less well-to-do resident of Cairo spends the three summer months.

Right now, a lot of the boys are very interested in breeding silk-worms. Most of them, of the little ones at least, have boxes full of these interesting creatures; they buy them from each other, and nothing amuses me so much as to see my little Jews discussing the current rate, or speaking of their partnerships with one another. I would never have believed they could really have such an instinct for business.

Talking of caterpillars, this is the season for the oleander hawk-moth caterpillar. One can often see its tracks, but it is not easy to find. So far I have caught only one, and it expired miserably. You can tell Guiguite that a cocoon of the mimosa-egger, the only one I had left, finally opened, yielding a small, dark grey, villous butterfly. However, I noticed it rather too late, and it had had a chance to get hurt as it flew.

Since my last letter, the weather has cooled off considerably. On Sunday I went off to those strange vacant terrains—partly rubbish heaps, partly cultivated, partly desert—to the south of Old Cairo. One spot in particular, where an old Arab aqueduct rises out of a rocky region to come to an abrupt stop in the middle of fields of good black earth, recalled certain etchings of the Roman countryside. One fellah, seeing me hammer a rock, was curious to find out what I was doing. When he saw the minute fossil which I had just extracted, he began shaking with laughter —and so did I, by the way.

These Orientals are big children, and I cannot forgive myself for not knowing Arabic; it would be so easy to make friends with them, and I am convinced that most of the prejudices come from the fact that we continually confront one another like statues, absolutely isolated from one another for lack of a common tongue. These people are good-hearted, and it would be easy to do them good, because they are simple and little used to being treated with consideration. After leaving my fellah, I met two others, but they were much more shy; they cannot often have seen Europeans. They followed us for a long time, their heads wrapped in cloaks, their eyes bright as a wild cat's, and seemingly transfixed with astonishment They didn't even call out "Baksheesh," which an Arab hardly ever fails to do when you meet him outside the city—and sometimes in the city too. As regards baksheesh (the word for tip, as you know), I remember how indignant Father Le Marois[1] was in January, when a trolley car employee said to him on his return from Gizeh: "You been to Pyramids? Give baksheesh!" The reason was splendid.

I can well believe that the people here must find our behavior, Father Bovier-Lapierre's and mine, somewhat odd. We are about the only inhabitants of Cairo to go around with sacks, hammers, etc.; moreover, the Arabs still believe in the philosopher's stone and continue to search for it in the most childish ways. The superior of an Orthodox Coptic (i.e. schismatic) convent of Upper Egypt told Mr. Fourtan one day that it was not fossils he was looking for, but stones to turn into gold. People say that the secret of transmutation was discovered in another Coptic convent in Upper Egypt, and that its doors have been hermetically sealed ever since.

I believe I told you that we had found old fragments of pottery bearing heraldic arms in the rubbish heaps of Old Cairo. The collection has made great strides, and looks impressive. I was surprised at the number of *fleurs-de-lis*. The trouble about these heraldic arms is that they were not always attached to a family, but to an office, which makes them less interesting. Father Bovier-Lapierre is much more enthusiastic about these things than I am, and I enjoy his excitement when we come across a fragment of marble adorned with Kufic (ancient Arabic) lettering.

[1] At the time an instructor at the St. Francis Xavier school in Alexandria.

Over here, it is even harder for us than for you to realize what the elections really mean. But it doesn't look good. I hope that the Puy-de-Dôme at least has gained a good representative.

I have received all your letters regularly, plus one from Biel.

Goodbye, dear Father and Mother, I kiss you and pray for you and the family.

Pierre

All sorts of things to Joseph. I urge him to probe the quartz veins in the granite.

19

Cairo, May 31, 1906

Dear Father and Mother,

Yesterday I received your letters of the 21st and 24th, which gave me great pleasure, except of course for the news of poor Guiguite's new trial, just at the best time for her reflectors, as she remarks to me. My congratulations, especially, to Joseph for his first steps in photography; I shall carefully keep the two negatives which Mother sent me; it is certainly an experience to have a picture of my godfather in front of the main door at Sarcenat. I thought it would amuse you, in return, to see my features in a tarboosh, as well as the faces of two of my students —a large, good fellow—a Copt—whose headdress I borrowed, and an Italian, much more vivacious than his meek aspect would indicate. I still have not given up hope of sending you a picture of myself with all the philosophy students, one of these days.

While I am on the subject, let me tell you that they have done very well; eleven out of fifteen passed, five out of six of them science students. The passing-out lists have not yet appeared, but the average is more than satisfactory. It is a pleasure to see how happy they are; these are still their first moments of elation, the oral examinations having concluded the day before yesterday.

Father Rector's birthday was not celebrated until last Sunday; it was in some ways very original. In the first place, it is customary for the students to bring gifts in kind, which are subsequently forwarded to the Little Sisters of the Poor—or their counterpart in Cairo. Two days beforehand the tables begin to be laden with the most varied offerings—wines, liqueurs, cigarettes, sugar-loaves, potatoes, and especially great quantities of macaroni. The nicest are the live animals: this year there were six geese and six fine sheep, all bedecked with roses. Sheep are the special gift of the rich landowners of the Upper Nile.

On the great day itself, all the teachers are invited to dinner, and it is quite an experience to sit at the same table as majestic sheiks in silken robes (galabiehs) and beautiful turbans. The great event of the day was the performance of *Voyage to China,* which drew an enormous crowd of parents. The actors included former students who performed with real artistry, as well as current students, whose main function was to sing in chorus, and who did very well. Lord Cromer attended a part of the play, which was presided over by the agent of France.

At the Alexandria school, which goes in for classics more than ours, Aeschylus' *Eumenides,* as adapted by Leconte de l'Isle, was put on the same day. Apparently it was very good too; but I think that Cairo people would react to such a subject rather as Europeans react to a play in Arabic. A rhetorician—an Egyptian, it must be admitted—told me that he did not find the music of *Voyage to China* attractive.

The day after Father Rector's birthday, Father Bovier-Lapierre and I took advantage of a holiday to explore the debris of an ancient, part Jewish, part Egyptian city named On. To get there you have to travel one hour by train northwest of Cairo; then, after three-quarters of an hour's walk through fellahin territory, you come to the debris without too much difficulty. The scene resembles that of all ancient Egyptian city sites. A layer of broken stones, and especially of crude potsherds, thick tiles and fragments of jars extends over an undulating terrain (or "tell"), substantially plowed up by excavations or by the efforts of natives in search of old brick fragments to use for concrete. Here and there stand ancient walls of sun-dried brick, built as they are still built to this day, then enormous slabs of Aswan granite covered with hieroglyphics, and slabs of alabaster. It does not amount to much, but that has not prevented certain experts from reconstructing a whole plan of the city, with all the measurements, in greatest detail. Unfortunately Maspero himself confesses that it is only imagination.

Father Bovier-Lapierre garnered a number of jar handles bearing Greek markings, and I was lucky enough to find a flint saw, a finger's length, its jags perfectly preserved. Maspero has taken a fancy to it, and it will turn up one of these days in the museum. Not much is known either about the period or about the function of these stone tools, often very artistically fashioned, which are found in various parts of Egypt. A likely hypothesis is that they were sacred implements, and that their function continued long after metals came into use.

Independently of its archeological interest, On is a very picturesque place. It is very typical of the Delta, with its fields of wheat and cotton, clumps of palm and mimosas, each of which shades a sakieh turned by a gamoosa; but it is already the edge of the Delta, and behind the green fields you see the first white dunes of the desert rising in the direction of Suez, breaking the monotony of the cultivated fields. On the very edge of the desert there is even a big sheet of basalt, identical with the one I discovered last winter, but quite actively worked by convicts. The inhabitants of On had already used the stone. Unfortunately it is a compact rock in which there is little likelihood of finding attractive minerals.

It will interest Joseph to hear that I have found some very fine celestite crystals in the desert, one especially, a hand's length, an arm's thickness. Unfortunately they are not very transparent. The same day, I found a beautiful thistle with a ball-like flower, quite like those in the flower-beds at Sarcenat, except that the very thin leaves were more or less reduced to thorns.

I forgot to tell you about a visit to an ostrich park, situated in the desert near Matariya. Several hundred ostriches were there, very well acclimated and very profitable to their owner, chiefly on account of their feathers; the large feathers are plucked in November, the black body feathers in May. The big ones are dreadful looking beasts.

Goodbye, dear Father and Mother, I kiss you as well as Toto and Joseph. I prayed hard for you all to Notre Dame du Port,[1] and I shall do so again this month to the Sacred Heart.

Pierre

[1] At Clermont. It was at the celebrated sanctuary of Notre Dame du Port that Pierre's parents used to attend early Mass together when they were at Clermont.

20

Dear Father and Mother,

In just one month the boys will leave for the long vacation, and their ranks are already thinning; in the Orient people have no scruple about leaving a month before term ends and returning a month after school opens.

The passing-out lists of the new May graduates have finally appeared, putting the final seal on the school's success. In the science section, we placed second and fifth, which is very good. The first place, I understand, is more or less reserved for government candidates, but I do not know whether this is a fact.

For the moment, the principal news here is the heat; for some days the thermometer has regularly hit 104 degrees at noon. But Mother need not worry about me; I am certainly among the people here who suffer least from this temperature. My only grievance is that the desert is now virtually inaccessible; gusts of hot air come from that direction. So Father Bovier and I are obliged to fall back upon the cultivated land, which we comb with admirable constancy. Unfortunately, probably because it was produced artificially, it is poor in plant life, and even insects are fairly scarce. For the most part, in any case, they hide as best they can by day, except for some such as the mylabrids, of which I have caught three types, and the buprestids. I have caught two of the latter, one dark violet, the other copper-colored with yellow spots, rather like an *octoguttata*. Iñes Bey was interested in the second; he had never seen one before. Neither was he familiar with a ptinus which flourishes in large families in an old pottery bed in the rubbish heaps, or with a desert helix which I had found on one of my trips last winter (the one on camel-back).

This week I am preparing a sermon on St. Louis of Gonzaga for the students, and also a procession in honor of the Sacred Heart, which is conducted with great solemnity despite the rather limited proportions of the courtyard and garden. I am reminded of the days when I was rehearsed for the same purpose in the big avenues of Mongré.

So you will soon have Biel back; I hope Yéyé gets a first in the orals.

Public opinion here is considerably roused over an incident which has just taken place in the vicinity of Cairo. The captain of a British regiment, marching from here to Alexandria on foot, according to annual custom, was beaten by natives, and another officer killed. Apparently these gentlemen had been shooting, and had taken the notion of aiming at a dove-cot, in the course of which operation a native woman was wounded. So the village went out armed with clubs. The affair will probably have no consequences, the British having nothing more to covet here for the moment than what they have. Anyway, for the past week Cairo has had to do without European newspapers; the printers had asked for improved conditions, so the managements decided to suspend operations until agreement was reached. The first to publish without the consent of the others would be subject to a £50 fine. Meanwhile, the combined papers put out a little daily summary of the news, on a hectographed sheet. It is quite a novel idea.

As in every good school, this is the month of the prize essays. Just as at Mongré we used to go to Jassans in the evening, so the boarders here go to Matariya for supper, where what they enjoy most is the pool.

I have not been to the Giza zoo yet; apparently it is very fine. As for monkeys, the only kind I come across quite often are those I see on the street—*Souakim cynocephalids;* they are very gentle, and have very silky coats.

I have received all your letters regularly, and I am happy about Guiguite's good news; but the Delphine affair must be very bothersome to you.

Father is mistaken to think that Egypt is scorched. The trees here—the mimosas, the lebbek acacias—are barren of leaves during only two weeks of the year, in May; and the fields, rather dry since harvest time, will turn green again when the Nile floods. The great enemy of verdure here is dust, which encrusts the leaves. The past month has seen the brilliant flowering of a tree imported from Madagascar, the *Poinciana regio,* very similar to the acacia (the learned Father Bovier says that it is a cesalpinid); it is covered with big, bright red flowers, in shape and size rather like nasturtiums. They are to be found in all the gardens.

Whit Sunday was first holy communion day here. Father Garraud gave the youngsters their retreat, and since I was free, I supervised them for a part of the time. Father Garraud was pleased to have someone from Auvergne with him, and for my part I was happy to give his youngsters some help.

We received the visit of a department head of the Ministry of Education, ostensibly come to inspect French education in the Orient. He had little right to foist himself upon us, and he must have realized this, for he virtually requested the permission to visit. Everything went off very well. When he questioned a little Jewish boy on the moral of the fable of the dog and the wolf, the boy replied: "It is better to be free," and he probably did not guess how much wit that answer contained. In seventh, he asked a youngster what he did during recreation; the boy replied candidly that he did not play, having lost all his marbles. Naturally, the powerful visitor declared that Father Rector would give the boy some marbles in his behalf.

Goodbye, dear Father and Mother, I kiss you as well as Guiguite and Toto, and I pray to the Sacred Heart for you all.

If Guiguite has time, perhaps she would paint the four-pronged carrion beetle for me in her next letter.

Pierre

21

Cairo, June 30, 1906

Dear Father and Mother,

As I do not want this letter to come much after Mother's birthday, I am writing it quite soon after the previous one; consequently there is not much news.

The period of big feasts is just over, and with it my concern about a sermon, which I delivered satisfactorily for the feast of St. Louis of Gonzaga, and about the procession of the Blessed Sacrament, where my altar boys gave a tolerably good account of themselves. The only trouble with the procession was lack of space; as on December 8, the British army was represented by a large group of Irish soldiers, who conducted themselves very well.

At the school, we have reached those last two weeks which drag out the end of a year already virtually completed; the prize essays and a good part of the examinations are over, and the students scattered. My next letter will be dated on the eve of, or the day after prize-giving. Then there will be two and a half months of vacation, including three weeks at Alexandria, right at the seashore. As I am in very good health anyway, Mother can be completely at ease about me.

One departure which will change my existence for the worse is that of Father Bovier-Lapierre, who is leaving us next week for the Faculty of Medicine at Beirut. I shall miss him. However, since in the past four years a faithful companion who shares my tastes has always turned up, I hope that this time, too, Providence will send a man of resource to Cairo. But at this point we do not know who will make up the new contingent for next year. As regards my assignment, I believe it is all settled; it is to remain the same.

Last week, we took advantage of a not so hot day to make a trip out to the desert. I killed my first horned viper there. It was sleeping under a stone, and I did not damage it at all. It is no bigger than our vipers, very short, but with beautiful yellow and brown tints, identical with those of the sand; moreover, its scales are not smooth, but rough, almost bristling. Its head, especially, is beautiful: very wide, with a very short nose, and two horns beneath which its eyes shine with extraordinary harshness even after death. Actually Brehm's sketches are very true to life.

I realized that day that the desert, which is lifeless by day, is filled at night with animals which emerge from every hole. A sandy wadi was completely furrowed with snake trails; and for 225 yards we followed the tracks of a big lizard whose paws had left a clear imprint between 3 and 3½ in. long; it was probably some varanian. But when the sun shines, all these creatures hide in the holes which are almost everywhere apparent.

I discovered here a book by Canon Belon, of Mans, on the fauna, flora and customs of Egypt, which is absolutely delectable; it belongs to a priest well versed in the history of the country. Father must certainly know it. I intend to read it from cover to cover. I noticed, among other things, a mongoose, not badly drawn, but whose tail, for lack of space, was placed above the animal; the author takes care to note that this is only a typographical device, and by no means a reality. One is sure to find in the book at least as good a story as the "solitary sparrow."

I have received Father's book on the voyage of the natives of Montferrand, and although he may remain skeptical, I can tell him that I find it interesting. I shall show it to the fathers here who come from Auvergne—Father Garraud and Father Huguet.

I am glad that Father has been to Amiens, and that Biel could go with him. I expect you will soon have Biel back, pending Yéyé's return. Meanwhile it is our poor little Guiguite who is doing penance.

Goodbye, dear Father and Mother, I kiss you as well as Toto, and pray hard for you.

Pierre

22

Dear Father and Mother,

So here we are with our vacation begun, yet despite my free time I am somewhat behind in writing to you.

Prize-giving took place on Monday night, according to the prescribed rites. The ceremony was held outside, in the shade of a big multi-colored tent which is used extremely frequently in Cairo. No important marriage or funeral occurs without these carpets with their red and yellow arabesques being hoisted to shelter the crowd of visitors who come to drink a cup of coffee. I stress these details because on the very same night all this display was to provide us with the excitement of a blaze. At about 10 p.m. (I should tell you that the tent had been erected right below my windows) I had the unpleasant impression of awakening in a room lit up by the play of flames. For some unexplained reason, the canvas was burning in great style, accompanied by the shouts of the Syrian domestic staff which populates the house. From my advanced position I indulged in the pleasure of pouring water on the blaze; anyway, the fire was controlled at once, and the whole affair remained more of a comic episode than anything else.

As I told you in my last letter, we are staying here until the beginning of August; on the 6th we shall go to Alexandria, where it is less hot but much more humid. The advantages of the stay there consist mainly in the change of air and the proximity of the sea. Unless I inform you to the contrary, go on addressing your mail to me to Cairo.

The days preceding the vacation were rather flat, with students reduced in number and excited at the approaching vacation. They were saddened by the death of a rhetoric student. On that occasion I had the opportunity to observe the vehemence of the expression of oriental grief. At the moment of burial, the women of the family let out piercing shrieks which could be heard all up and down the street.

The weather is cooler now; unfortunately the middle of the day, from 10 a.m. to 3 or 4 p.m., can hardly be used for trips on account of the sun, which prevents me from exploring the area as I would wish. Nevertheless, I made a fairly long trip to find some scorpions on a slope which seems to specialize in them; but we returned with a frightful thirst. I console myself by combing the tamarisks and mimosas.

I am waiting with some impatience for the impressions or final results of the examinations.

I was happy about Françoise's news; you can tell her that I certainly did receive her letter from Tourcoing.

You have probably heard of the Tree of the Virgin, at Matariya.[1] It is a very old sycamore fig, descended, so the story goes, from the tree which shaded the Holy Family in Egypt. Half the trunk split last week under the weight of the branches, and what remains is not very impressive. A shoot will naturally be planted, but it will not have the same majesty. The tree stands in a garden belonging to the khedive, but we have free access to it. The khedive, who is out for anything he can get, wanted an exorbitant price for the site of the tree.

Goodbye, dear Father and Mother, I kiss you, as well as Guiguite and the boys, and I pray hard for you all.

Pierre

[1] See Michel Jullien S.J., *L'Arbre de la Vierge à Matarieh,* Paris 1904.

23

Cairo, August 5, 1906

Dear Father and Mother,

We are leaving tomorrow morning for Alexandria, and to ensure regularity in our correspondence I think it a matter of elementary prudence to write to you before we leave. We are not going to Alexandria itself, but a couple of miles to the west, near Ramleh, to the school's country house. I had a glimpse of the place last year; its great advantage is that it is right at the shore—which is really almost the only attraction of the trip. Alexandria is dull compared with Cairo; but I console myself easily with the prospect of familiarizing myself with the algae, molluscs, etc. of the Mediterranean. There is also the desert, which begins to the west, relatively close. I am curious to see what it is like—it must be extremely flat; but I must have the right companion. If only Frédéric de Bélinay were still there! I think I told you that he was at Canterbury.

These first two weeks of vacation have gone by very peacefully. The weather has been quite tolerable (barely exceeding 95 degrees), though turning increasingly humid because the Nile is due to reach its maximum spate early in September. I expect to see the Delta tomorrow in all its splendor, with the cotton fields in flower, and already quite extensively flooded.

Two trips to the Mokattam hills, with some of the students, netted me a big celestite crystal the size of a fist, and a harvest of prehensile fish teeth (shaped like a cat's claws) of which little is known as yet. Mr. Fourtan will examine the latter; meanwhile I have sent the former to a minerologist of the museum who had asked me for some of the substance. In connection with museums—I am religiously collecting chrysalids for Mr. du Buysson; quite a number of them are to be found against the sun-dried brick walls which so often occur near villages, and there are some quite beautiful types. I intend to send my finds to Mr. du Buysson on my return from Alexandria, where I hope to complete them. I have again found some interesting insects: a little metallic green buprestid on the mimosas, and another of the same color, but the size of a water beetle, on the tamarisks. The latter is not uncommon. Right now, there is a profusion of big, black cetonia speckled with yellow; they are very pretty, and are particularly partial to the henna tree, from which the natives extract the tincture with which they paint their nails red.

Turning to another field, this week, for the first time, I saw the big black and white kingfisher which Father told me about early in the year in connection with the Saxicola. There were three of them over a canal, hardly shy at all, and getting a good catch, for these canals teem with fish.

I also visited the ruins of a very old Cairo mosque; they consist chiefly of minarets—round towers, but curiously enveloped half-way up by a thick square tower, in such a way that between the two there is a space about 2½ yards wide. This is probably due to the fact that the mosque borders on the ancient ramparts which can be followed for a considerable distance along an exterior watchman's beat, and along another, interior one, which is vaulted and very well constructed. Hundreds of bats haunt the top of the spiral stairway leading to the tower; they hang everywhere, and the heaped up excrements give off an odor such that, the claims of science notwithstanding, I had to beat a retreat. From the outside, one has a magnificent view of the old sections of Cairo, bristling with minarets, traversed by winding streets crowded with camels, watermelons, sheep, Arabs. All this movement seen from high up, far from the native smell and singularity, was doubly curious to observe. This mosque, like many others in the city, is being restored. It is a good policy, for the Turks made some very beautiful things there.

Recently I read a book which is very interesting for anyone who has seen something of the East—*Les mémoires du marquis de Nointel* by Vandal. Most of the customs observed in Constantinople at the time of Louis XIV are still to be found here today.

To go back a little further, I made a second visit to the Museum of Egyptology. Like all museums, it is a whole world, and one emerges reeling. The great new show-piece is the Hathor cow, about which Maspero is apparently enthusiastic. It was discovered last winter near Luxor. Hathor was a goddess worshiped under the likeness of a cow; statues of her had been found before, but none so big or especially so beautiful as this one. It is life-size, painted red and white, and really marvelously true to life. Petit-Jean would be prostrate with admiration. Young King Amenhotep is shown suckling eagerly.

I have received all your letters regularly. I expect Joseph and Biel have received mine. Naturally, I thought a lot, yesterday, about you and my little goddaughter;[1] may she protect the family.

[1] His little sister, Marie-Louise, who died on August 4, 1904, at the age of 13.

Goodbye, dear Father and Mother, I kiss you as well as Yéyé, Guiguite and the others, and I pray hard for you.

Pierre

I enclose two stamps which Toto and Gonzague may not have.

As I told you, the best is that you should write to me to Cairo.

24

My Dear Little Mother,

You seem to be so convinced that I am completely exhausted that I wish this letter could take only one day to reach you at Sarcenat to reassure you. I keep racking my brains to think what I could have said in any of my letters to give you that impression. Actually, I am very well, and I repeat that the heat did not bother me at all.

I am writing to you from a terrace, 65 yards away from a very blue sea, where I take healthy dips as early as 5 a.m.; and there is always a cool breeze. It would be sufficient to restore one after a whole year at Khartoum.

You can tell Guiguite and company that I am collecting some fine insects; I shall send them the descriptions in due course.

As you see, this letter is an immediate answer to yours of the beginning of August, in which you express your concern. I think it will reassure you.

I was happy to hear that Joseph had some ideas about his future; in his place, I should be glad that the October test is so close. With a little composure, he should be able to bring it off.

I take this opportunity to wish you a happy feast of the

Assumption. You can imagine how I shall commend you all on that day to the Heart of the Blessed Virgin. A year ago we were together; those good days will return when the Sacred Heart wills it; that does not stop me, meanwhile, from loving you dearly. I kiss you, as well as Father, Guiguite and the boys.

Your child,

Pierre

P.S. Failing everything else, don't fall back on my poor hand-writing. I am writing to you under conditions which are most unfavorable to calligraphy.

25

Dear Father and Mother,

We are now two days from the end of our vacation and the beginning of our retreat; but that means still another week here, in the fresh, cool, sea air, which has made my August more pleasant, perhaps, than yours. The retreat is to be given us by Father Mazoyer, whom I had not seen again for a long time; it will call up old memories, and I expect we shall speak more than once of Clermont.

These two weeks have naturally passed quickly, and I have spent most of the time at the seashore. I have only two things against this shore: the first, if I may so express it, is that it lacks a distant horizon, since, unlike the desert, which one imagines as continuing right through Africa, one knows that it is bounded by the somewhat banal shores of old Europe; the second is that it lacks any considerable tides. The few yards which are uncovered are not sufficient to enable one to collect all the riches of which the waves bring only fragments. Nevertheless, I have collected quite a good assortment of shells, which are very useful to know in paleontology, many of the types cropping up as fossils, especially in the relatively recent layers, as at Mokattam. I can identify them thanks to a collection left by Frédéric de Bélinay. Sea-urchins abound in the

111

rocks, but one has to go out quite far, and get into the water; I found only one. The coast consists of hardened sand, sufficiently compact for the sea to erode and dentilate it like real rock. Consequently the approaches to the coast are covered with reefs. The long lines of reefs, parallel to the coast, and riddled with deep holes, make these waters dangerous, and from my point of view act as wards against the best and largest of the deep-sea shell-fish.

Yesterday I saw some natives fishing—illegally—with dynamite. They moved forward on a breakwater of rocks and finally spotted a shoal of fish, into which they hurled a cartridge. The cartridge immediately exploded, and they collected at least thirty fish, the length of half an arm, slate-colored, with longitudinal black stripes, about as broad as carps. I do not know their name. The epilogue was the arrival of thieves who threatened to denounce the fishermen, and had them give up some of their fish to them, then the arrival of a Negro coast-guard whom they persuaded to close his eyes to the affair, and finally the appearance of a shark, which never fails to turn up, so I am told, after an explosion, to get its share. At that point I had unfortunately already left the scene; this was regrettable, for since the shark ventured into the waters immediately adjoining the coast, it was seen only a few yards away. An Englishman went into the water with the coast-guard's rifle, but the shark disappeared. Apparently it was the kind known as a sand shark, which is not more than 2 yards in length, but can easily bite off a hand or leg. It is common here.

Last week I made a trip as far as Agami, west of Alexandria, where the development of the city is stopped by the desert, which begins at Mex. On the way there, we followed the sea along a flat beach bordered by a kind of pasture land and a few little palm copses. I was surprised, as I crossed some ditches filled with rushes, suddenly to hear the loud clamor of crickets which live there in their hundreds and which our passage had disturbed. In Cairo, there are few crickets; they are small and sing discreetly. Those at Agami make a terrible racket, like the ones in Provence; this was the first time that I had seen them like this on low plants.

At Agami itself, there is a little old dismantled fort; Napoleon I landed there. That is where civilization ends; all one can see now are the chalk-white dunes extending to the horizon, bordered by waters rendered a fluorescent green by the very white sand which forms the sea bottom. And it must go on like that as far as Tunisia. On the way back, we crossed the tongue of land up to the top of the little rocky ridge overlooking Mariut. At this time of year, the lake is very low, and surrounded by a broad band of white and sparkling salt. Since the water is nowhere much deeper than two and a half yards, the slightest lowering of the level uncovers large surfaces. I had thought that work was in progress to reclaim it; actually all that is being done is to maintain it at a specific level. To reach the rocky ridge, we crossed a small lagoon, dry at this season (see the "map"), full of salt and tiger-beetles. What was most wonderful were the colors—dead white sand, with long, greenish or red trails in the wet and saline parts, the whole bordered by the dark blue of the sea.

The region of Sidi Gaber is less picturesque and much more luxuriant. Where it is not cluttered with villas, there are magnificent orchards of fig trees and date copses. For beautiful things in that area one would have to go to Rosetta, or at least to Abukir, but I shall probably not do so this time.

We went out in the port twice in a sail boat, which is great fun, on account of the large number of steamers which come and go.

There are few birds here, even on the sea; from time to time one sees some large dark birds with light breasts, but even with field glasses I was not able to distinguish them clearly. Near Lake Mariut, on the other hand, I saw a wader in flight which I think was really an avocet; in any case it reminded me forcibly of the sketches in *Wild Spain.*

This is the place for chameleons; they quickly become sociable, and eat flies with enthusiasm.

All your letters have reached me on time, and I sympathize with you in your dry spell. I shall think much of you and the family during this coming week, asking our Lord to bless us all. You know how much I continue to love you. I am very well (for Mother).

Pierre

P.S. My letter is being mailed late. This has enabled me to take a turn beyond Ramle. I take it back: the countryside *is* very lovely, with its date palms standing in the white sand dunes.

26

Dear Father and Mother,

So here I am, back in Cairo, and not unwillingly, despite the charms of the sea. We left Sidi Gaber on the very day the retreat ended, taking with us from Alexandria one of my best friends, Father Tissot, who is going to teach here. Since Aix, we had not been separated except last year. I shall not be able to make particularly long trips with him, but he will singularly enliven school life for me.

Did you know that Christian Burdo was going to Beirut to study oriental languages? But he is going by way of Constantinople, so that I shall not see him this time.

From now until the time school opens, I shall leisurely prepare my course for next year; I have new subjects to prepare, which is quite pleasant. However, I do not yet know whether I shall have to teach the lower classes, third and humanities, as last year. Meanwhile I get about quite a lot, sometimes in the line of duty, to show new arrivals the wonders of Cairo (the desert has rather fewer admirers), sometimes, and especially, on my own account, since my duties are constantly growing. I am becoming a supplier of shells, neuroptera, orthoptera, chrysalids, lepidoptera, etc., not to speak of making a fundamental study of geology, or rather, paleontology.

Mr. Pallary, of Oran, has responded to my first package; he advises me about shell collecting, asks me a number of things and has returned to me, classified, the types which I sent him. Among them is a new kind of desert snail. Unfortunately I was not the person who found it, and the priest from whom I got it cannot remember too well where he picked it up, so that it is hard for me to find more specimens, which are eagerly sought after. Sturdy snails are not uncommon in the desert, but the types seem to keep very much to themselves, each one occupying a particular region to the exclusion of the rest. Hence the best way of finding any new ones is (invariably) by going farther afield. And that is not at all easy.

Egypt is at the peak of the flood period, and also of the date harvest; the little date forest of Marg offers a spectacle of extraordinary animation. Arabs have moved under their trees to gather the dates; they live there with their families and their chickens. To climb the date palms, which are often very tall, they use strong ropes which they tie around the trunks and on which they sit; by doubling up and placing their feet on the jagged protrusions of the trunks, they climb up very fast.

For the first time, I have been to see the Nilometer, which for centuries has measured the water level of the Nile. It is merely a catchment, communicating with the river, in the center of which there stands a marble column serving as an indicator, in addition to several scales carved in the sides; all around the catchment is an inscription in Kufic (ancient Arabic) lettering. Three or four bench-marks give the average altitude of the place as 29 meters. The Nilometer is at the southern end of the little island of Roda, on the outskirts of Cairo. The island is still only partly cultivated and in some areas quite wild; we happened upon a filthy mud village, to the terror of the children, who scattered in confusion together with some white chickens which had been painted carmine. Fortunately an Arab directed us across the tip of the island, which is covered with lovely gardens that exhale a fragrance of henna, with arcades of lemon, orange and guava trees.

You will have learned from the papers of the death of Prince Ibrahim, who was killed in France where he had gone on a pleasure trip like all wealthy Egyptians. His funeral took place the day before yesterday with great ceremony. I was lucky enough to see the cortège pass in a big street near the Citadel, in a marvelous setting of mosques, and among purely native spectators. First, some mounted police (shaweeshes), then five or six camels laden with large cases from which Arabs took various things and threw them to the crowd. Presumably because it was the end, the only things left in the cases were pears, which did not prevent a full-fledged assault on the last of the camels, the one least protected from the crowd. I also saw more than one pear spurting up on the backs of the distributors. Behind the camels came three gamoosas, whose lot was to be sacrificed forthwith on the tomb, then distributed among the spectators. Then came a long line of soldiers, and finally another line of men in tarbooshes and multicolored aprons carrying what looked like censers and large chiseled dishes filled with flowers. Finally came the representatives of various groups—officers, priests of different rites, consuls, and, curiously enough, whirling dervishes, with ascetic features and immense pointed hats of grey felt. The coffin, drawn by eight horses on a gun-carriage, was followed by members of the family, and by a long train of coaches, virtually hermetically sealed, carrying Moslem ladies. It was a sad end for the poor prince; he was quite young, a very rich proprietor of large estates near Alexandria, and, apparently, on very cold terms with his cousin, the khedive.

I have received all your letters. I wish you good hunting at Vialles. Yesterday I spoke to an Arab at Marg, who told me that he had fired forty rifle shots that day on water fowl in the rice paddies; all he had actually bagged was five or six snipe, but they were beautiful ones. One was the *Rhynchaea capensis* (female, with a ginger-colored head), which Shelley portrays on page 250. He called it a golden snipe. The others, which he called royal snipe, looked like large snipe.

Goodbye, dear Father and Mother, I kiss you fondly, as well as the family. I shall pray hard for you tomorrow, the 8th. You know that I am with you on these last anniversaries of Albéric's death.[1] I am quite well.

Your child,

Pierre

Many thanks to Guiguite for her letters, particularly for that of the 31st, which has just reached me. I hope poor little Mother will have found her glasses again quickly. It will interest her to know that the Sacred Heart[2] had a house-warming the other day in their new building. (With the cook from the rue de Varennes!)

I am quite well.

[1] Died at Sarcenat, September 27, 1902.
[2] The convent of the Madames of the Sacred Heart.

27

Cairo, September 26, 1906

Dear Father and Mother,

I am a little late in writing to you, and when this letter reaches you Biel will have left, and Yéyé will probably have learned his fate; I confess that I await the result with some impatience. So tomorrow is Albéric's anniversary, which as usual makes me think even more about you, about your eldest children, about the old days; despite its sadness, the 27th becomes a family feast day. With you, I shall ask our Lord and the Blessed Virgin to have each one of us accomplish as much good as possible, by the means they want. Albéric and Loulou will obtain that for us.

Here, too, the school year is about to begin; the opening date is October 3. For me, things will be much the same as last year—at least exteriorly, for I no longer suffer the secret anguish of the very beginning. I am still to teach physics in third, humanities, rhetoric and philosophy. This time, however, each class has an altogether different program, whereas last year many parts of the courses were common to several classes, since a new program of studies was being introduced which included subjects that were equally unfamiliar to very different classes. I benefit from this in that I no longer have to repeat the same experiments at least twice, which was tiresome, and that I shall

119

now teach certain new items which I shall thus have the opportunity of exploring further. Of course, the students of rhetoric and philosophy in the science section are the only ones to have a fairly interesting program; there will be five of the former, three of the latter, which is not disquieting, and will make it possible to work very agreeably for the students. Beginning this year, there will be two types of Egyptian (baccalaureate) examinations: one in the humanities, the other, as before, in philosophy. However, at this point we have hardly any brilliant candidates to present, and our successes next May will probably not match those of four months ago.

I have seen a lot of Cairo these past two weeks. To begin with, I revisited Saqqara in the capacity of a guide to a passing priest; I enjoyed the trip more than in January, and for two reasons: there were only the two of us, and we were therefore very much at ease, and our trip was taking place at floodtide. We covered the six or seven miles separating the station (Bedreshem) from the Pyramids on donkey-back, along a causeway set between two seas of reddish water, out of which there emerged only the mud villages on their islets, and the tall date palms with their yellow clusters of which there is a real forest, planted on the ruins of Memphis. The flood waters stop right at the foot of the sand cliff which marks the beginning of the desert and the site of the necropolis. On the causeway we passed a solemn Arab wedding procession. Following the established rite, the bride, hermetically sealed inside a multicolored palanquin, was borne by two camels, preceded by flute and tambourine players and men on horseback armed with rifles. Along the way, I saw an all-green bee-eater perching (*Merops viridis*). This is the migrating season, and if I walked in the fields more I should probably see many of them.

I saw the Serapeum again, with its immense slabs, and the tombs covered with rustic or hunting and fishing scenes: baskets filled with fish where you can recognize the Nilotic types, crocodiles, hippopotami, cynocephalids on leashes, cheetahs used for hunting, etc.

We returned on donkey-back to the Giza Pyramids, which is not very interesting; as soon as you pass the ruined Pyramids of Abu-Sir, you have to skirt a cultivated area (the part without pencil hachures; the rest is desert) which is unattractive. The trip took three hours.

Last Saturday I visited a meteorological observatory at Helwan, the only one of its kind in Egypt (quite well equipped by the British). Among other instruments, I saw a seismograph, which the day before had registered two small tremors. Helwan is a gloomy town, established right in the desert for the benefit of tuberculars, to provide them with absolutely dry air. Thus, there are few trees, just houses, closed like tombs, built systematically along deserted avenues which cross at right angles—a real checker board. I believe it is more animated in winter. It has sulphurous waters caused by the decomposition of gypsum beds.

Yesterday I went a long way west of the Pyramids, in search of fossils. We traveled on donkey-back. The Libyan desert is dreadfully monotonous; pebbly undulations as far as the eye can see, broken here and there by wadis, the caravan route to the big troughs of Fayoum or Natrun. We reached a mountain mass of limestone rocks (cretaceous), full of faults, its seams furrowed or collapsed; I came back richer, among other things, by two fine sea-urchins.

Last Thursday I succeeded in penetrating as far as the big yellow dunes north of Matariya, beyond the Marg palms. They are formed of marvelously fine and undulating sand, whose golden tints stand out brilliantly against the blue of the sky; it is like an ocean of great rolling waves. On the way, I passed the tracks of a flock of large birds, runners evidently, probably bustards.

Dr. Iñes Bey has just left on a trip through Eritrea with

121

two companions; they were armed with guns, butterfly nets and hammers, and resolved to return laden with booty. It seems that in Abyssinia there are the following zones: hot and arid, up to 1,300 yards; luxuriant and African up to 2,500 yards, alpine and fairly poor beyond. It is the second, of course, which they are going to explore. Apparently it is springtime there now, and everything is in flower. I shall give you details of the results of the expedition in November; Iñes kindly invited me to come and look at them, which I shall not fail to do.

I returned to El-Akim, the mosque with the bats, with Father Tissot; for two hours we explored from top to bottom, without an Arab to bother us; just imagine an old castle rising in the very middle of an Arab town.

Goodbye, dear Father and Mother, I kiss you as well as Joseph, Guiguite, Toto, Gonzague.

I shall write to Guiguite next time, or even sooner.

Pierre

P.S. At Jersey, Gonzague will find a rather old Father Loiseau who was my great friend here all year.

28

Dear Father and Mother,

I was naturally delighted about Yéyé's success. In addition to having an assured career, this will make it possible for him to be with Biel again and to avoid the critical prospect of another year in the postal service. May the day of glory dawn for our good Joseph too! Biel wrote me a note from Paris, which I answered, enclosing a word of congratulations to his roommate. They are really nice boys, and I can well believe that the triumphs which have marked their return to school cannot really console you for their absence.

Here the fatal date of October 3 does not have the somber externals of our vacation-end at Mongré or elsewhere. Apart from a few tears of fright shed by the very little boys as they pass from the hand of their father to that of Father Rector, homesickness is uncommon in this cosmopolitan country where there is little sense of family. I have the same classes as last year, with this advantage, that I have been relieved of the "third," and after the first days of getting things going I think the school year has got off to a good start. I am interested in my rhetoric and philosophy classes in the science section. In any case, as you know from last year, the students start reviewing at the beginning of March, which means that for the teacher the school year ends. One of my students, the most brilliant of the lot (a French boy), dreams of the Centrale.

The last days of the vacation were rendered agreeably eventful for me by the arrival of one of my friends from Mongré, Jacques Roullet, who stopped in Egypt on his way home after three years in Indo-China, where he works for the Ministry for Water and Forests. He was doing science when I was doing rhetoric, but we knew each other well, and I spent some happy hours showing him around Cairo and having him tell me about Tonkin. He had not met Uncle Georges at Hanoi, to his loss. His job at the moment consists less in selecting and planting trees than in discouraging the nomadic natives from burning what already exists. To that end, he makes a number of tours of inspection, which are not the least pleasurable features of a position which makes him virtually sole representative of his administration in the country. He assured me that the colony was beginning to flourish, and that it was just at the right stage for our competitors to take it away from us—which, he added, would be easy.

So far I have had less luck with Claude de Rivoyre; he sent me a note from Toulon asking me to write to him at Port Said with "tips" on how to get to Cairo. The *Alger* should have passed through the Canal around the 7th, but I have seen nothing arrive. I do not despair, however, because it seems to me unlikely that if he had found it impossible to come, Mr. de Rivoyre should not have sent me a card from Port Said or Suez.

Last Sunday, I went to the foot hills of Mokattam to take my mind off my first classes. In addition to picking up a remarkable sea-urchin fossil, this provided me with the enjoyment of a magnificent view: it was an evening lit up by the beautiful colors of the Orient. The walls of Mokattam and the Tombs of the Caliphs were burnt gold, the heights purplish-blue, and the whole city was enveloped in lilac dust.

Some days previously I had seen the same spectacle from

the top of the minaret of Ibn Tulun, one of the most curious mosques of Cairo, whose immense quadrangle, surrounded by porticoes, can be reached only by going through purely Arab sections. From the top of the tower you overlook the huddled terraces of the native houses, and their little gardens enclosed by high walls, topped by clumps of palms. One might just as well imagine oneself in Timbuctoo.

I was quite unaware that Father Mulsant[1] was related to the de Villeles. He is in very good form and charming, which is not without importance, since the teachers have almost as much to do with the prefect as the students. The day before yesterday, he and I went on a donkey-ride in the Marg palm forest, in search of photographs; he is a great photographer since, as you know, he is a "cinematographer." The hardest thing, and also the most amusing, is to catch the Rebeccas as they very romantically carry or wash their pitchers. Fear of the evil eye, and *a fortiori* of the lens, will long remain very strong among them. Nevertheless, we did find some Bedouin women who posed of their own accord among their goats. This earned them a piastre, which they accepted, of course, in a corner of their veils, to avoid contact with strangers. These Bedouin women have the odd custom of attaching all the coins or medals they possess, sometimes of gold or silver, to the veils which cover their faces right up to their eyes. Thus they often carry a veritable coat of mail which must be uncomfortably heavy.

To my delight, I have resumed responsibility for an "omnibus," and I have an interesting route which enables me to enjoy the contrasts between the Continental or Shepheards' Hotel and the swarming throngs of an Arab street, through which one drives at the risk of bumping into a shop front or its lamps, and of crushing the impudent youngsters in their galabiehs

[1] Father Alfred Mulsant (1866–1943) was prefect of studies at the Cairo school at the time.

who lay regular siege to the footboard. My clients include a very little boy who goes on waving goodbye to his mother and his little brothers so long as his house remains in sight; it is very touching.

We finished with the really hot season long ago, and the weather in September was very pleasant; as usual, October has its periods of heat. Yesterday, for instance, it was 89 degrees, and today will be the same. But it is the end; anyway, I am very well.

Goodbye, dear Father and Mother, I kiss you as well as Guiguite, Joseph and Toto, and I pray for you.

Pierre

The Assumptionists' pilgrimage stopped at Matariya. It is briskly but very well conducted, and the pilgrims' garb is not too odd, which is worthy of note.

I enclose two stamps for Toto.

29

Cairo, November 1, 1906

Dear Father and Mother,

I have just received, with Mother's letter, the news of Joseph's splendid success; you must all be very pleased about it there, especially the party concerned, who will probably begin by treating himself to some fine woodcock shooting to make his happiness complete. Now he will have to decide on a position in society, and I shall be quite interested to learn of his decision.

Here, life during the past two weeks has been marked by the fruitful monotony of the "regular order," extending indefinitely, which is the period when the students really work; the year is now in full swing, and everyone has adjusted to the unbelievably complicated timetable resulting from the diversity of subjects—Arabic, French, English, science, etc. Arabic, especially, encroaches deplorably; by reason of the programs, students have to spend half their intellectual forces learning a literary language, entirely made up of formulae, which is not without analogy to Chinese characters. It is a waste of time which is hardly compensated by its services to national vanity. However, the "regular order" was interrupted the day before yesterday to give place, according to custom, to the students' retreat, which closes tomorrow. For despite the date at the top of my letter, I am writing to you on the 31st. These are of course three days of vacation for the Moslems and Jews. Since they constitute the bulk of my passengers, I conduct a half-empty car rather pathetically through the streets of Cairo. Right now, anyway, those streets are hard to negotiate; paving, and even tarring, is proceeding everywhere, the administration having happily chosen to carry out its program at the very time when Cairo life is starting up again with the arrival of the first tourists. The hotel terraces are beginning to fill up, and each evening the youngsters whom I take home gaze happily at the guitar players, the pianolas and even the Arab acrobats who besiege the cafés.

A week ago we had some quite violent storms, following a period of considerable heat. There was a great deal of lightning, but with extremely weak rumbles of thunder, I am not really clear why—and very heavy rain. Since I was making a trip in the desert on that day, I could watch the beautiful light effects on the thick clouds moving across the sky. I reached a little station on the Matariya railroad amid swirling dust, just as the shower started. Even the train was not a secure shelter; the rain came through the cracks in the carriage roofs, and the compartments were flooded.

That day, I went through the big construction works of the "Oases." This is the name of two little garden cities which a big Belgian financier is having constructed right in the desert, close to Cairo, about half-way from Matariya. Each little garden city will be isolated from all other habitation; the houses composing it will all have gardens and will have to meet certain hygienic and esthetic standards. An electric railroad (of the Metropolitan company) will operate the run to Cairo. The project is admirable, and so far one of the oases had been laid out. The first thing to go up is a gigantic hotel. A happy point —there will be a Catholic church in the very center, very well situated, at the express wish of the founder of the enterprise. The question is whether fashion will second the undertaking;

for this is the essential condition of success. Apparently there has already been frightful speculation, as everywhere in Cairo now on sites where building is proceeding. Work on this has been going forward for some time now, but I do not think I have mentioned it to you before.

Finally, Mr. de Rivoyre did not come after all; I thought afterward that it was rather brazen of a midshipman to expect to leave his ship for a day or two in order to look around Cairo.

Iñes Bey has not yet returned from Abyssinia, but I think he will soon. Apparently he was received there with great ceremony, which is just what he feared when he left. I hope that this will not have impeded his movements.

Ramadan is now in full swing; we notice it only from the rows of lamps surrounding the minarets, and from the small lamps which children carry in the streets. I have sometimes chanced to pass through a native quarter just after the Citadel gun has signaled the close of the fast (at sunset). The streets were crowded with outdoor vendors of provisions and fried foods, but it seemed to me that the Arabs' first thought was not to eat but to smoke a good hookah. That is the fasting which they seem to feel most.

I was shown a motor boat on the Nile. Oh Memphis! There were none last year, but it is a sport which will catch on, of course.

Goodbye, dear Father and Mother; my congratulations to Joseph, and my thanks to Guiguite for sending me Yéyé's note. You may be quite sure that tomorrow and the next day—perhaps especially tomorrow, since Albéric and Loulou are surely in heaven—I shall be united to you with all my affection. I kiss you.

Pierre

129

30

Dear Father and Mother,

Yesterday and today I received the letters in which you tell me about Joseph's plans, and it seems to me that everything is for the best. I think the choice of a special physics teacher particularly fortunate; the mathematics program absorbs all Croze's energies, and I still wonder how I managed to pass my science examination with what I knew of physics and chemistry. In any case, Mr. Croze will come to belong to the family; remember me to him when you see him. I was touched by Yéyé's cult of the Sarcenat apples; he has not changed since the days when, wearing the famous cap and carrying a stick under his arm, he inspected the meadows after the evening "lesson." As for Gonzague, he sounds to me like a deplorably lazy fellow; let us take consolation in the thought that Albéric, if I am not mistaken, did not work much harder at Mongré. Do tell him that not to take more trouble is the best way for him not to get into the navy.

During the past two weeks, the regular order has continued to prevail; the program for the year is beginning to be seriously breached. Next week there will be tests for all the senior classes; this means more papers to correct, but less teaching.

Just now, apart from occasional morning fog, the temperature is delightful; this is Cairo's fine weather season. It is the right moment to explore the desert, and I take every advantage of it, despite the dearth of companions from which I have suffered since the departure of Father Bovier-Lapierre. Last Sunday I managed to get quite far in the el-Thy wadi, a big fault running south from Cairo to the Gulf of Suez; I was rewarded by the discovery of a very pretty little helix with festooned whorls, similar to a type noted at Alexandria. I immediately sent it to Oran.

The return journeys, especially, are marvelous, on account of the sunsets; all the slopes, whether of rock or of bare earth, take on tints of burning bronze, extraordinarily warm, and it is no mean sight to see the sun disappear on the horizon of the other desert, with its jagged line of Pyramids. I wish you were here to see it. The day I found the helix, darkness overtook us when we were still an hour's journey from Cairo, and all we had to direct us were the two long minarets of the mosque of the Citadel, each surrounded by two circlets of electric lights, lit up during Ramadan. They served as two great lighthouses.

Ramadan closes the day after tomorrow; we shall see the big flocks of sheep, which insolently push their way through the busiest streets, regardless of traffic, being led to the slaughter houses. Everyone eats mutton to celebrate the end of the fast, which will be marked for the residents of Cairo by the return of the khedive.

I was forgetting to tell you about the two big scorpions I caught. They adorn my table, each in a jar. When they extend their tails and claws, they are about as long as one of the lines of this letter; they are greenish yellow, and look dangerous. I shall rear them for a while before pricking them. When a scorpion wants to eat an insect, it grasps it in its claws, folds its tail back over its head, and gives it a smart tap.

Right now, there are a great many large bats here, as big as

131

nightjars; in the evening they circle around two fig trees in front of the school, uttering cries which sound like a loud creaking. They eat leaves, of which one finds the chewed remains. The unfortunate thing is that, as soon as the food is swallowed, it is digested, and large brown spots literally stud the façade. At Matariya, a whole row of mulberry trees alongside the chapel had to be cut down to prevent this additional plastering. I should like to get hold of one of the offenders. I am told that one of the servants here, whose name is Abd-el-Malak, or "servant of the king," is able to make them come flocking to him by imitating their cry; but I have not yet put his talent to the test.

You will have read extracts of Charlot's report on the schools in the Orient. Criticism could hardly be more petty, and the points he stresses are a manifest avowal of his inability to find any serious fault. The substance of his anecdotes—judging by one, at least, which we could recognize—seems to be true, and there has inevitably been imprudence in matters of detail. The facts he cites are the result of an inquiry which he had the audacity to conduct among any students he could find who had been expelled. These he describes as courageous deserters; in fact, they swell the ranks of the French secular school here—a wretched school (partly through the fault of the director, who is said to be absolutely incapable). On one page of his report, Charlot has the indelicacy to poke fun at a musical performance of the students in fourth which he had been allowed to attend purely as a matter of courtesy. It is not very pretty, or very true.

Goodbye, dear Father and Mother, I kiss you as well as Joseph and Toto, and I love you always. I hope there will be plenty of woodcock. All along the Nile, apparently, water fowl abound, but one would have to have a boat or go into the marshes of the Delta or Fayoum to know it.

Pierre

31

Cairo, December 7, 1906

Dear Father and Mother,

I have received all your letters on time, and it is I who am behind in answering. Anyway, it is good that I should be writing to you on the eve of the Immaculate Conception, for it gives me the opportunity to tell you that I shall pray hard to our Lady for you and the family tomorrow. For me, the feast day also involves a solemn Mass tomorrow, and a procession at Matariya the following day. But I am beginning to be sufficiently used to directing the altar boys not to let it worry me too much. Like last year, the procession will be made up of students and the best Cairo society, arriving by automobile (for there is a motor road from Cairo to Matariya, as there is one from Cairo to the Pyramids, and these are the only two), by carriage or by train. But this year the staff of the French agency, with its beribboned cawas (gentleman usher) will not be there to grace the ceremony. Mr. de la Boulinière left for Athens last week, and his substitute (Mr. Klobukowski, the son-in-law of Paul Bert) has not yet arrived. Mr. de la Boulinière's departure is a great loss to the school, and his successor will probably reflect only very faintly his character of a true French gentleman. I believe he left without too great regret, for the French colony is being split from top to bottom thanks to the efforts of a masonic group. Mr. Klobukowski is of course as little religious as possible, but he is intelligent, so one hears, which will perhaps suffice to make him a defender of religion. Mr. de la Boulinière came to take leave of the school; he concluded his farewells by granting a holiday which, according to custom, will be added on to the new year's vacation.

A week ago, I went to visit Iñes Bey, who talked to me for two hours about his travels in Eritrea. His only unpleasant memory is of Massawa, a terribly hot and humid city; beyond that point, the country is ideal. Between the altitudes of 1,200 and 2,000 yards there extends a kind of plane on which plantations of cotton, vanilla and coffee have been started. From the train to Asmara, one can see flocks of gazelles and bustards running, and it seems that in these regions one can also find a type of boa. Iñes Bey, who is primarily an ornithologist, went further, to the 2,500-yard plateau which precedes the high mountains. He describes it as magnificent and precipitous territory, covered with forests of euphorbia, the floor of which is carpeted with wild hyacinths and geraniums, and populated by bands of cynocephalids. These are usually friendly, except that they sometimes throw stones or, if they are too deliberately driven away from a particular spot, they rush there and start digging with rage, as though to look for what has been hidden from them.

The plateau is furrowed with great veins of aurific quartz, exploited in beggarly fashion by some penniless Italians. There are also iron ore and copper mines, the latter formerly exploited by the Portuguese.

Among the birds he brought back, whose names I unfortunately do not know, since they had not yet been labeled, I noticed these especially: a gigantic black tucan (boceras . . .), more than a yard long, armed with a beak wider than a hand, apparently a denizen of the rocks; another tucan, black and white, much smaller and quite common; a big, pinkish-brown roller; two or three speckled woodpeckers; a collection of dazzling hummingbirds, which live among the aloes flowers; a widow bird, with interminably long tail feathers; some kingfishers, one with little metallic feathers adorning its head, rather like the New Guinea bird of paradise in Buffon's book; a little falcon quite black; two big ringed plovers; a kind of green hocco; a black lark (untufted) with carmine tail-feathers; an Abyssinian partridge and an Abyssinian francolin.

I saw nothing near the whole collection; I shall complete my visit some other time, when everything has been labeled. This method of preserving birds simply by stuffing them with straw is not only readily available to anyone, and fast (Iñes prepared all the specimens he killed on the very same day), but it is also very convenient if one wants to amass a large collection in a small space and to study the specimens, which are very easy to handle in this way.

The lepidoptera which he brought back (mostly diurnal) were still in their paper wrappings. There were some fine coleoptera, buprestids, cetonia, mylabrids, and especially an enormous click beetle with big pectinate antennae. I was particularly interested in some minerals from the auriferous regions.

The Eritrean natives are apparently very gentle, and marvelous climbers. Their churches, instead of bells, have sounding stones with a very fine tone. One of Iñes Bey's companions brought back a whole collection of Byzantine-type icons, not very artistic, but at least curious. Abyssinia proper is an inaccessible and absolutely closed country; its capital, which the geography books talk about, is a peripatetic city which moves with the Negus wherever there is wood. As a matter of policy, there are neither

135

railroads nor highways. The only facility is the telephone, which the Negus reserves for his own exclusive use during the first part of the day.

The great luxury in Eritrea is the possession of a European hat; Iñes Bey saw a native proudly wearing the paper covering of a top hat.

To sum up, he returns with the impression that Eritrea is a country as marvelously rich as it is unknown by Italy. The chief engineer of the steamer, who has been going to Massawa for years, compared it to a desert island in the Gulf of Suez! What, then, must Italians think who have never even been within sight of their colony?

By comparison, Egypt seems pale; nevertheless I enjoy it more and more. My trips in the desert are becoming a real pleasure. Recently I collected quite a number of fossils, including a large fragment of shark jaw. I also came upon an assembly of six big vultures making a meal upon a dead horse. I am not sufficiently versed in the species to identify the one—or ones—to which these belonged. In any case, I was struck by the accuracy of the sketches in *Wild Spain* of birds at rest as well as in flight.

One small Cairo news item: the sacred carpet is to leave the mosque of the Citadel tomorrow for the annual pilgrimage to Mecca.

When this letter reaches you, Guiguite will probably be in Cannes. This yearly separation must be hard on you, and I grieve for you. Our Lord will take account of all these sacrifices which he imposes on you.

Thank you for Mlle. d'Arcy's message; I was greatly moved by it, as you were. Goodbye, I kiss you with all my heart.

Pierre

My Dear Guiguite,

This letter will surely find its way to you in Cannes. I shall write to you there; meanwhile, be sure that I always think of you.

My big phalaena caterpillars are doing well—I have eight of them!

Pierre

32

Cairo, December 22, 1906

My Dear Father,

I am very late in writing this letter to wish you a happy birthday, and I doubt that the Indian mail will bring you my letter until a couple of days after Christmas. At least you will know that I did not forget you on that day, and that I asked God as best I could to bless you, you and the family. I need hardly repeat, need I, how much my heart is with you, especially as I realize better the quality of the life you provided for me until I was eighteen. It is those years that have earned me all the rest; and, from another point of view, I doubt that one could be happier on earth than I was during that time. I honestly believe that all of us, your children, can say the same . . .

By the same mail I send you a little publicity brochure which may interest you by reason of the information it contains about Egypt. I am sorry that it does not include a general view of Cairo; I shall try to find one for you on a picture postcard.

On December 31, I am going to accompany some students to Minya, south of Cairo. You will find the name on any map of Egypt. Others than I might be very sad at the prospect of stopping half-way to Luxor; but around Minya there are some little-known calcareous mountains where I hope to collect fossils. I shall write you my impressions of Upper Egypt.

Christian Burdo,[1] more fortunate than I in that respect, left us last night for Thebes and Aswan, which he is to visit on a vacation trip with a group of other students from the university of Beirut. It was a real joy for me to see him again so unexpectedly. He left me, for a few days, three albums of photographs of Jersey which brought the cliffs right back to me. Last year, apparently, near Plémont, he came upon a spot riddled with rabbit holes which were inhabited by puffins, and in one of them he was able to capture a live *Alca torda.*

The new French Minister, Mr. Klobukowski, arrived yesterday.

Goodbye, dear Father, I shall stop now so that this letter may leave this morning. I kiss you as well as Mother and Joseph and Toto. Happy birthday.

Pierre

[1] Father Christian Burdo (1881–1961) always remained one of Father Teilhard's most faithful friends. Like him, he was an enthusiast of scientific research. He was professor of cosmology and anthropology at the scholasticates of Jersey, Vals and Chantilly, and scientific reviser of the philosophy archives.

33

Dear Father and Mother,

Here I am, back from Minya a few hours ago; there is one evening of vacation left, and I hasten to take advantage of it to tell you something of my trip.

First of all, everything went off very well; decidedly, the more one sees of Upper Egypt, the more one likes it—and I had never realized so well as this time how exquisite are its jungles of sugar cane and its plains of flowering berseem or beans. Since my objective in going there was to do geology, I spent most of my time exploring the "mountains"; but the best deposits happen to lie right at the foot of the cliff bordering the Arabian desert, on the very edge of the fields, so that the scene of my work lacked the austerity of the desert. Most of the time I was prying sea-urchins from the limestone with my feet in the black silt of the Nile. The gamoosas and camels, and especially the fellahin, stared at me, of course, wide-eyed, and a worthy Arab, thinking that I was digging for "antiques," asked to see my research permit. The temperature was very mild, and only twice was I too hot; that was when I was right in the middle of the rocks.

As I told you last year, it is very easy to reach the Arabian desert from Minya; once you have crossed the Nile on some boat with a big triangular and acute-angled sail, there is only a half-mile of fields to cross before arriving at the white wall bordering the plain, and these fields are so luxuriant and so pleasantly dotted with palms that it is a pleasure to walk among them.

Quite a few jackals lurk in the mountains, and we chased two of them for some time; since one of us had a gun, they might have had a bad time of it but for an over-cunning move in which I acted as the beater. They popped up under my feet, and took off in the wrong direction.

One morning I also glimpsed a very large bird of prey, which seemed to me to have a white head; it was apparently leaving the mountains to go hunting, and it was escorted by two or three crows which seemed to be following in its wake to get the pickings. Iñes Bey told me that eagles were not uncommon in the Nile valley, particularly the imperial eagle; he has killed a number of them around Cairo. It seems that once they alight on the edge of the fields, they no longer pay the slightest attention to the desert and are content to survey the plain, so that one can approach them from the rear very easily.

To return to Minya, I made one trip, yesterday, to the Libyan desert; it is a two-hours' journey on donkey-back, and at that spot it consists solely of shifting dunes, which enclose a number of lagoons bordered by the inevitable dwarf tamarisk. The sight is a very curious one, and the place must be teeming with water fowl, but I did not have time to explore it very thoroughly. There, again, the route was almost as interesting as the objective.

I saw and crossed Bahr Yusuf again, on whose banks a small vulture was meditating; and I had a close look at the fellahin villages. One of them was completely Coptic-Catholic, and we were received with open arms. I have already described these villages to you: an accumulation of low houses built of dried mud, set on slightly higher ground to beat the flood, with palms for shade. All around are fields over which hoopoes circle, as well as flocks of hoplopleuras, bee-eaters and swallows. As soon as you get to Minya, you come upon pigeonries; these are mas-

141

sive, rectangular structures, topped by a forest of earthenware pots and mud niches where the pigeons take shelter.

The Coptic village priest I told you about is a worthy man, with a bronzed face and a small black beard; he is a former student of the Propaganda in Rome, and is happy to remain in his obscure little village on the edge of the desert, living in a mud dwelling which is something quite unbelievable. All the Coptic priests are in that condition, and their churches too; this particular priest happens to be a really saintly person, and keeps up his church (!) and his rectory (!!) to the best of his ability. The church is as large as the drawing room at Sarcenat, and the back of it serves as a school. Yet I am not sorry for the fellahin or their priests, except in regard to their lack of education. Despite their poverty, their life is much more peaceful and patriarchal than that of our peasants in France. But perhaps I just don't know them well enough.

One day we took the train as far as Siut (or Assiut), far south of Minya. It is a pretty little native town, built at the foot of the Libyan chain, which at this point has become much higher. On good donkeys, we reached the little village of Deir Drunka, a few miles farther south, where there was a school to visit. It is in the wall of rocks overlooking Deir Drunka that you find the caves of Lycopolis, inhabited at one time by solitaries. Until quite recently, natives lived there like troglodytes; but the Department of Antiquities made them decamp, and now earth houses have risen alongside the fields, at the foot of the mountains.

While one of my companions, better versed in Arabic than I, was questioning some children, I climbed over the rock wall, but I did not find many fossils. From up there I could look down upon plateaux blackened by the ferrous patina of the deserts, whose slopes filled out the horizon to the west; some Bedouin trails presumably led to the Kharga oasis. To the east, the view was more cheerful; there, the valley is completely planted with berseem and beans, with no visible boundary between the fields;

nor is there a single tree. Thus from one desert to the other, apart from a few excrescences marking the sites of villages, there was a single pale green ribbon, completely unbroken. At Drunka, I saw a doom palm. I don't think many more are to be found farther north, though the garden at Minya has one.

During my entire trip, I did not concern myself with antiquities at all, though they abound in the region; everywhere one comes across *koms* of black earth and brick, on which villages are usually perched—Oxyrhincus, Hermopolis, Antinoë. However, I did go to the last-named place; it used to be a powerful Roman town, and somewhat later the neighboring caves, in the mountains, came to be filled with solitaries. There remains a vast expanse of ruins, with a few columns, between the Nile and the mountains. Egyptologists do not fail, moreover, to visit the very old hypogeums of Beni-Hassan, and the ruins of Tell-el-Amarna. I did not go, for lack of opportunity; and probably, if circumstances had brought me into their vicinity, I should quickly have deserted them for the nearest rocks.

Finally, this morning, I took the train back to Cairo. Despite the monotony of the journey, it is always agreeable to see the pyramids go by one after the other: Maydum (near Fayoum at Wasta), Lishte, Dashur, Saqqara, Abusir, Giza. Moreover, the canals bordering the tracks are always full of big black and white kingfishers, sandpipers and hoplopleuras which are in no way distracted from their occupations by the passage of the train. I never weary, especially, of watching the hoplopleura, whose plumage is of supreme elegance: black wings, brownish-grey plumage, black and white throat and breast. The kingfishers, like the bee-eaters, are particularly fond of telegraph wires; I have seen as many as four perched side by side, watching the waters.

Now I am back in Cairo, which seems quite noisy and unpleasant after the little provincial town where one heard little more than the sound of a muezzin and occasionally the siren of a cotton mill or a Cook's steamer. I close my letter on the 8th.

Today is the anniversary of the day the khedive ascended the throne (?), in honor of which the principal streets are lavishly and garishly decorated, concerning which the French papers, which pride themselves on their taste, will not fail to register a protest. I am supervising an essay for which my students seem to be more or less vainly collecting their ideas—distant now by a week's vacation.

I have received all your letters, and even a very long one from Françoise. I was amused about Yéyé's misadventure and his test; it is hard to imagine his leaving school out of stage fright. And yet, basically, it was that. I am very happy about the goods news concerning Marneffe. Yes, I know Father Dugout very well; in fact, I know hardly any man whose life has been rendered more eventful by travel, sports and politics. Father Chauvin's[1] visit honored me, and I recognized in him Guiguite's boldness; but I believe that at that time he was not more informed than she was herself as to my future destination. My fate depends essentially on a "replacement."

Goodbye, dear Father and Mother, I kiss you with all my heart, as well as Guiguite. I love you and pray for you. I forgot to ask you to convey my best wishes for the new year to my godfather and his family. Lots of good things especially to Marie.

Pierre

P.S. The sea-urchins I collected at Minya apparently include some new and interesting specimens. I shall tell you more about this when I get more detailed information.

[1] Father Louis Chauvin (1861–1937) was twice Provincial of Lyons (1906–1912 and 1918–1924). Father Auguste Décisier (1878–1963) could say of him: "He spread peace everywhere. His mere presence was a living sermon on the Christian ideal."

34

Dear Father and Mother,

I was very sorry to learn about Biel's illness; it calls up too many memories for you not to be doubly painful, and for the poor little fellow it is hard to have to lose a year of Centrale. Let us hope that our Lord will turn this to some advantage, even for his future; in any case, we know that from the point of view of heaven—the only one which will count one day—it is for the best. But you must suffer a great deal, and really, the good Lord leaves you little respite what with Guiguite, and even Gonzague. There is reason, here, for much confidence in him who directs everything, and perhaps also much coin with which to expiate for the country; if it is really this that our Lord has in view, it is a great honor for the family. I pray much for you all, and I might almost say quite specially for Yer-Yer and Guiguite; the latter must be worried, and the former must feel very lonely, after living in companionship last term. Judging by Mother's letter of the 10th, I can expect news of convalescence by the next mail; may it be speedy.

There is little local news to give you, for after all last month's events everything is quiet. However, the day before yesterday we received the visit of the new agent, Mr. Klobukowski. He spoke in very frank and liberal tones, much more categorically than

Mr. de la Boulinière[1] would have dared do in public. He desires unity and virtual disregard of the divisions existing in France. It remains to be seen whether his hand will not be forced. He granted the customary holiday, to the great joy of the students. Mr. Constans lauded Father André[2] to him, which may make many things easier.

You will find more news in my letter to poor Biel. I want to have time to write to him before the mail boat leaves tomorrow.

Goodbye, dear Father and Mother, I kiss you. It seems to me that I love you more in these circumstances.

Pierre

[1] Diplomatic agent and consul-general of France. In his address he said: "I wish the different students of this French school to see in me only a friend."

[2] Father Albert André (1872–1919) had just arrived in Cairo, where he succeeded Father Côtet as rector of the school. He came from Constantinople. He was subsequently superior of the Armenian Mission, of which he had published a history (Paris 1900).

35

Dear Father and Mother,

I think that Mother is again going to find that I am behind in writing; but the days go by fast, and I am horrified to see that my last letter was dated three weeks ago. The last days of Shrovetide, which followed soon thereafter, were spent in the customary manner. Taking advantage of the projector, which was still there, there was more cinematography, but this time with amusing films, which had obligingly been lent to us. Despite our students' assiduity in frequenting the cinemas of the city, they had a lot of fun at the showing here.

On Shrove Tuesday I set off, as I had intended, to the Lybian desert, a little south of the Giza Pyramids, and I returned with a good haul of fossils. There are some quite recent strata there (pliocene), dating from the period when the lower valley of the Nile formed a fjord filled by the sea, where one can find hundreds of scallop shells which look as though they had been deposited by the last tide. Oysters of this type are still to be found in the Red Sea. Since there had been a strong wind on the previous day, I found, in the rock crevices, several butterflies which had been driven off the cultivated fields. I shall talk to Biel about it, in answer to his letter. From now on I shall look twice before considering a type as belonging to the desert fauna.

I am also zealously continuing with my digging in the Mokattam hills. These past two weeks I have made the periodic and compulsory round of the quarries bordering Cairo, and I came back with some nice things, including a remarkable sea-urchin. The quarrymen pick up some samples, but almost solely shark's teeth, because they are shiny, and only big ones at that. As is customary, they want exorbitant prices for them, but are prepared to follow you, progressively lowering their demands.

Last Sunday, however, I went on an archeological expedition to Old Cairo together with Father Tissot[1] and the cream of his students in third. It was fun for everyone, and the youngsters displayed a laudable desire to learn about the history of their city, of which they are completely ignorant. You probably are not aware that modern Cairo stands on a site selected in three successive stages: there was Babylon (Old Cairo), Coptic and Roman; Fostat, ruined at the time of the Crusades and buried under the debris which extends between Old Cairo and modern Cairo; and finally present-day Cairo. Old Cairo is therefore an interesting place. I returned to the ancient Coptic churches which I had visited in September with Mr. Roullet: Sitti Maria, with its crypt in which, according to tradition, the Holy Family stopped, and "el Muallaka," a little jewel of Arabic art, with three cylindrical vaults, filled with delicate inlays, sculptured ivory and old icons.

Our visit to the old mosque of Amru (a big, square court, with a deep colonnade on one side, a fountain in the middle and two minarets with two quoins) was very gay. There are two columns there very close together, known as the "trial" columns,

[1] Antoine Tissot (1880–1959), rector of the schools of Mongré and St. Étienne, then preacher at Grenoble for twenty-five years in succession. He died at Grenoble.

and if one squeezes through one is saved. The boys rushed on them like a whirlwind (just for fun, of course); and I have rarely laughed so much as when I watched the procession; only two had to give up the attempt to squeeze through the space. The mosque is now deconsecrated, so that we were able to indulge in this irreverence without interference.

Further on there is another miraculous column, said to have been transported from Mecca by a heavenly hand; you can see the Prophet's name written *in* the rock. In September, I made a mistake, noticing only an engraved inscription; the real one is actually inside the marble. It must have been produced by effecting an internal rupture of the marble, for instance, with a heated point.

Finally, we went to see the old Nilometer. The orchard surrounding it was not filled with the perfume of henna and guavas, as in summer, and the level having gone down, the column which serves as an indicator was almost completely exposed. A bench-mark shows an altitude of 20 metres at this point; it is low.

I have seen a lovely book here on Cairo, recently published, which cannot be very expensive: *Les villes d'art célèbres. Le Caire* by G. Migeon, Librairie Renouard, 6 rue de Tournon, 1906. If Father gets it, he will probably find it very interesting.

This week I am completing my program with the philosophers; there is only review left now, until May, when the examinations take place. Moreover, we expect hot weather again. Ten days ago, we had one of those hot, dusty winds which occur only at the edge of deserts. The atmosphere seems filled with thick, grey fog; actually, it is a layer of fine sand, rising up from the ground, which stings the nose, and through which one can still make out a vaguely blue sky. But Mother need not worry; the real heat does not start until the end of April—and I repeat, I do not suffer from it.

149

Goodbye, dear Father and Mother, I kiss you as well as Biel, Joseph and Toto. Gonzague has probably left you. Tell Marie that I congratulate her heartily on Jacques, and that I pray earnestly for his welfare.

Pierre

36

Dear Father and Mother,

This is Passion Sunday, which takes me back, like you, I am sure, eight years ago. This month of March evokes so many departures, and on the 7th, too, I did not forget Albéric. He protects us now; as for Françoise and me, you know how much our hearts remain with the family, and how happy we are in the lives we have chosen. That is the beautiful part of all these separations, and in the end only that part will remain; but now we are still at the stage where one feels the pain, and I wish it could be softened for you by our affection.

Here, the most important thing is that Easter is two weeks off, so there are tests, examinations, and for me the preparation of the Holy Week ceremonies with my altar boys. Not that I am very busy, actually. Since my first days as a teacher, I have never felt myself so much in control of my teaching, so that most of my classes, at least those with the senior students, are sometimes positively pleasurable to me. And then the greater part of the year is over, and the beginning of May will take away the philosophers.

During the Easter vacation I shall probably make an excursion to Fayoum, an oasis southwest of Cairo, famous for its fossils and also for its place in antiquity; Lake Moeris is there, and

Antinoë. I think I shall enjoy that exploration a good deal, and I shall describe it to you in detail.

Meanwhile, I have been through Arab Cairo again; a second archeological expedition took place with Father Tissot and the cream of his class, who are virtually the cream of the school. This time, there were no "trial" columns, but nice things to see. First, the Bab al-Zuweila gate, vaulted, flanked by two towers from which dethroned caliphs and crusaders used to be hanged, enchased now in the heart of the Arab quarter near the very beautiful mosque of Al-Muayyad; the heavy swing doors, studded with large nails, are covered with dirty little rags, testifying to the public gratitude to "saint" Zuweila, whom half the passers-by venerate by pressing their heads against the door. An old witch insisted that this was an infallible remedy for headaches. Next, we visited the big mosque of Al-Hassan, near the Citadel. Its walls are enormously high, somewhat reminiscent of the exterior of the palace of the popes at Avignon. Restoration work is under way, but it will be hard to restore it to its primitive splendor; one of the ancient doors, made of bronze worked with silver and gold, is on exhibition in a kind of wall-cupboard. We ended our tour with a visit to the Ibn Tulun mosque, about which I wrote you in September. It is the oldest of the Cairo mosques still standing, and one of the largest in area. It was built by the famous caliph, Ibn Tulun, who slept floating in a lake of quicksilver, and it is certainly majestic, with its immense courtyard surrounded by porticoes decorated in a style that is still severe. If Father sends for the Migeon booklet, he will find more information about it.

These visits to mosques are doubly interesting because life still goes on in the setting in which they were first built. I was recently reading an account by an Arab poet of a trip on donkey-back to Old Cairo, in 1240; his description of donkeys and the habits of donkey-drivers could appear without alteration in the travel notes of a Cook's tourist. As for the fellahin, they are still living in the times of the pharaohs.

I was present this morning when a pilgrimage returned from Mecca, according to all the rites. I think I told you that each pilgrim is escorted home from the station in triumph, in full Arab regalia, and often riding in a buggy. My man this morning was nobly seated on horseback, preceded by two camels bearing a palanquin, then by a grotesque personage wearing on his head an object that I can compare only to a cornucopia or to an elephant's trunk, then by two more camels carrying two warriors brandishing swords, then by strangely attired dancers performing wild but at the same time elegantly rhythmical dances, and finally by two more camels on which children were perched beating kettledrums as hard as they could. For such occasions, the camels are very strangely caparisoned: heavy red materials with designs in gold hang down like sheets at the rear and at either side of the animal, as well as on both sides of its head, which is surmounted by a plume. Under all this, they continue to ruminate with shifty looks, slowly turning their heads, with their great black shining eyes, in circular motion, but always on the same plane. The whole procession moved slowly into the street which passes in front of the big hotels, obstructing traffic, but to the delight of the tourists, probably. The touching part of the ceremony is to see the natives crowding around the holy man returned from Mecca to kiss his hands; there is something very religious and very noble about it.

We are still enjoying the beautiful, cool days of spring; last Thursday there was a bold attempt at a south wind, which did not last. I was in the vicinity of the Mokattam hills, and I witnessed the curious sight of a sudden, violent whirlwind passing 250 yards away, churning up the sand; I could hear its whistling, but I did not feel a breath of it. Five minutes later, it is true, a cloud of dust arrived which cut off the view beyond a few yards, and filled one's eyes.

153

This is the beautiful season in the desert; almost everywhere, on the floor of the wadis, there are flowers—yellow crucifers, geraniums, thick-leaved sorrel. These flowers do not form a continuous carpet, but they suffice at points to perfume the air. In those parts I flushed a big hare, which was not very shy, and which I let go three times in succession; the first time, I thought I was dealing with an animal the size of a jackal, so misleading are the proportions of objects where there are no trees to serve as a basis for comparison.

Goodbye, dear Father and Mother, I kiss you and pray for you all. Today, the 18th, is Biel's birthday, and I did not remember to write to him. I hope Cannes will do him a lot of good. Tell Guiguite that I expect to write to her very shortly.

Pierre

37

Cairo, March 31, 1907

Dear Father and Mother,

So I leave tomorrow for Fayoum. As I expect to write to you on my return, I shall be brief this time, but I must at least give you some news of myself.

Our vacation started yesterday, after a Holy Week in which ceremonies and examinations went off well. To inaugurate the vacation, I wandered all last evening through the bazaars and the old Arab quarters, in the company of Father Tissot, who is enthusiastic about them. We began with a visit to the Arabic museum, which I had not seen before; it contains jewels of marquetry and embossing, big lamps of enameled blue-green glass from mosques, many wood sculptures (arabesques), fragments of vases bearing the coats-of-arms of caliphs, such as one still finds in the rubbish heaps; but the absence of any picture of some kind of life renders this whole accumulation of beautiful things lusterless, especially in a city which possesses the Egyptian Museum.

To avoid a shower, we turned into a narrow alley of the bazaar, where we found a jeweler's shop richly stocked with precious stones. After showing us an uncut emerald as big as a fist, on which he placed the exorbitant price of £25,000 (it is of dubious "water"), he informed us that he was a former

155

student of the school, and went on to tell us that he intended to spend a season in France, in Auvergne! As he spoke of La Bourboule, I told him that it was indeed the most picturesque resort he could select in central France. This encounter in the heart of the maze of bazaars was quite amusing.

In order to get some information about Fayoum, I returned to see Iñes Bey and his birds; the little white vulture which abounds in Upper Egypt is the *Percuspterus aegyptiacus*.

On the subject of natural history, and in answer to another of Father's questions, the sea-urchins are interesting for a variety of reasons: there are so many kinds; they are very characteristic in themselves, and of the sites where they are found; finally, they constitute a long series whose transformations are very interesting to follow. I may bring some back from Fayoum, though the region is interesting primarily for its vertebrate fossils.

I received Mother's letter today; Biel had told me about Guiguite's grippe, and I am glad that it is not serious. I think of Toto's imminent departure; let us hope that Gonzague will realize that he owes him an example of industry. So there goes the last little one . . . It must be hard for you. Do you intend to go to his first communion?

Goodbye, dear Father and Mother, I kiss you, as well as Guiguite and the boys. I shall write to you, then, at the end of the week. I pray for you.

Pierre

38

Cairo, April 9, 1907

Dear Father and Mother,

I am just back from Fayoum, which shows you that my stay there was a long one—a week. On my return, I found your letters of Holy Week, with Biel's about Monaco; I am glad they gave him such a good reception there. Now poor Toto has left you; life at Sarcenat, without a little one, will seem very different for you . . .

Here is some information about my expedition; you can use my map to follow it, or better still, maps which you will probably find in any fairly complete atlas. It will be simplest to give you a day-by-day account.

Easter Monday. Left at 8:30; arrived at Medinet el-Fayoum about 11:30. You see that it does not take long; one leaves the main Luxor line at the Wasta station. The train quickly plunges into the desert, and after twenty minutes or so it descends into the oasis. You know that in ancient times (right at the beginning of known history), Fayoum was a depression completely filled with water; now it is all drained, except for Lake Larun (Qarun), which is still 50 miles long and an average of 6 miles across. Of course, the exposed area is extremely fertile, but in the central regions the landscape is fairly uninteresting, with relatively few palms, big wheat fields as far as the eye can see, and the circle of mountains barely visible from Medinet el-Fayoum. Fortunately I did not remain there all the time. We[1] were somewhat perplexed as to how we were going to manage, in a very Arab region, where hotels are few, bad, and unreasonably expensive. Then we made the acquaintance of a former student of the school, a rich Copt of the area, who piloted us around Fayoum for a week; incidentally, he was ignorant of many parts of the territory.

The first evening, we went to see the ruins of Arsinoë (Crocodilopolis) which border on Medinet. They resemble all the old ruins of Egypt—an expanse of blackish earth forming several hills (*koms*), literally covered with potsherds. The natives exploit this earth as fertilizer, under the supervision—unfortunately insufficient—of the Department of Antiquities, which by no means appropriates everything that is discovered. At Arsinoë, the ruins are very extensive, and since the town was still flourishing in Greek times, there still remain many house walls which are slowly being brought to light. The houses must have been low, and in any case very close together; they were all built of sun-dried brick made with Nile mud. That is still the way people build here.

In general, the ancient sites of Fayoum are of interest only to specialists; a great deal of papyrus, Egyptian, Greek and Coptic, has been discovered there. But there are no magnificent ruins, as at Luxor, for example.

That first day we made a number of visits, in particular to the Coptic Orthodox—that is, schismatic—bishop, a venerable old man (alas, very ignorant; since the Copts do not want married bishops, and since their priests are all married, they get their bishops out of the depths of the monasteries) who received us squatting on a divan and smoking a pipe (chibouk) 2 yards long. These past few days I must have drunk on average at

---

[1] There were two of them on the excursion: ". . . he, an expert in hieroglyphics and I, an ardent geologist" (*Relations d'Orient*).

158

least ten cups of coffee a day; it is true that the cups are small, and the coffee excellent—aromatic, and as thick as cream. Our host was still observing Lent, since the Coptic Easter falls only in a month. The Copts, especially the Orthodox, observe excessively rigorous fasts, lasting nearly half the year; during the Lent preceding Easter, eggs, butter and fish are forbidden. There is exaggeration here, especially in the idea of fasting as the principal act of religion. In any case, no attempt was made to subject us to this diet, since Easter for us was already over.

Tuesday. In the morning, we visited Bihamu, where one can still see a causeway with two great pedestals formed of heaped-up slabs on which two colossal figures of Pharaohs used to stand; they have since disappeared. In those days, the water came up to the edge of the causeway, and it is believed that these were the "pyramids" which Strabo claims to have seen in the middle of Lake Moeris. He had probably come there when the Nile was in flood . . . On the Bihamu side, Fayoum is very pretty, because it is wooded. There are big fields of fig trees, gardens with vine arbors (Fayoum is famous for its grapes and its poultry) and many date palms. After taking coffee with the *omday* (native mayor) of Bihamu, we returned to Medinet, then left for Lake Qarun. A half-hour's train ride (as far as Ibshawai), and an hour and a half's ride on donkey back, brought us to a little hotel, or rather, a hunting lodge (on the map, at the place marked "huts"). A hotel has put up four or five large huts on a strip of land in the midst of rushes; they are very comfortable, and include a small building covered with an awning for cooking and meals. From there, one can enjoy the view at one's leisure, listening to the frogs in the rushes and also to a kind of warbler which sings loudly and well. To the north, toward the desert, the lake comes to an abrupt end, and right away the chains of mountains and plateaux rise in tiers one above the other. On the Fayoum side, by contrast, there is a wide, marshy belt, full of tamarisks and rushes, where the natives spend their days fishing a species of fat carp. These three successive planes—the dark green marsh, the blue lake, the yellow mountains—make a marvelous picture. We spent the night there; it is known as the Moeris Hotel.

Wednesday. Early in the morning, we crossed the lake in a strong boat. Every moment, herons and big snipe rose out of the rushes; at the point where the swamp gives place to deep water I saw flocks of coot and duck. They were everywhere, like black dots covering the water, sometimes coming so near that one could make out their colors. Here and there, pelicans could be seen swimming about majestically; they must be hard to approach; I was lucky enough to see four of them taking flight at once. In that connection, I observed that Shelley has a few pages on Fayoum; they will inform Father better than I could on the birds of the area.

Upon landing, we made our way to the ruins of Dimê, then to the little Greek temple of Qasr-el-Sagha, six miles further on. All around the lake you find traces of the sites of ancient Greek cities, indicated only by the undulations of the sand or sections of walls. Now the desert has taken over completely. As we neared Dimê, the chief of the *gâfirs* (custodians) of the Department of Antiquities, who was with us, noticed two Bedouins digging, which is absolutely forbidden; he finally got them, but after quite a tough struggle, in which he had to use guile. The Bedouins began by threatening him with their guns, so he passed himself off as a mere tourist guide; it was only after some of our boatmen had joined us that he fell upon the offenders and disarmed them. Bedouins are the scourge of Fayoum, and sometimes make it unsafe.

This trip was my principal objective. Above Qasr-el-Sagha, the mountains are very rich in fossils, and a half-day's camel ride further, around Jebel Qatrani, a whole bed of remains of great mammals has been found which scientific expeditions periodically exploit for the benefit of museums. Unfortunately

I had very little time, in view of our distance from Qasr-el-Sagha. However, I brought back a large shark's tooth, and many specimens of a strange fossil altogether peculiar to Fayoum; it is not really known to what type it belongs. In its complete, or rather, reconstituted form, for only fragments are to be found, it is between four and eight inches long and broad. It is known as the Kerunia Cornuta. We did not return to the "huts" until about 7 p.m., after a delightful crossing; it was calm, and the water milky. We slept at Ebchawaï, which we did not reach till about 10 p.m. It was pitch dark, and our donkey caravan, consisting of my companion and myself, the two diggers and three armed *gâfirs,* presented a very pleasing appearance of "adventure."

Thursday. Excursion to the Hawara and Lahun Pyramids. An old horse-cab, a discard from Cairo, served as our means of transportation. For two and a half hours we traveled along a fairly narrow road bordering the Bahr Yusuf, a curious little river which rises near Asyut, follows the Nile in a parallel course, and empties into Lake Qarun. Its water is everywhere channeled off to water the fields, and at Medinet it is divided into five or six streams which radiate outward to fertilize the whole of Fayoum. Fayoum's existence depends on irrigation, which is marvelously contrived there.

For a few piastres, our host bought a store of fish from some fisherman operating on the banks of the Bahr. The fish appeared much more varied than in Lake Qarun: eel, silurus, fish with mouths similar to the famous oxyrhynchus of the ancients, etc.

The Pyramids, which are more recent than those of Giza (they date from the twelfth dynasty), are far from equalling them in majesty. They are no more than about twenty-one yards high, and built entirely of sun-dried brick fashioned from Nile mud. This gives them an unusual blackish color. Near the Lahun Pyramid are the debris (that is, as usual, heaps of

161

potsherds) of the guardian city of the Pyramid. Interesting finds of papyrus have been made there.

Some way further on is a little *deir* (convent), right in the desert; three small white cupolas rise from an earthen enclosure. It was recently restored by an Orthodox Copt, and is now a place of pilgrimage. Formerly the only access to it was by means of a rope over the wall of the enclosure, as is still the case at Natrun and at the convents of St. Antony and St. Paul (in the latitude of Fayoum, but toward the Red Sea). Now there is a door. As I waited for the key, I ate some raw beans which my donkey driver had presented to me (the fellahin love raw beans), and watched an astonishing colony of worker bees which populate two walls facing north, forty yards long by eight or nine high. There are thousands of them, harmless, completely engrossed in building their honeycombs.[1] Since they have been at work, they have created a layer of silt which may be over some 30 inches thick. This represents the work of several centuries. A strange country, where such labor can be pursued without interruption.

Next to the Hauara Pyramid, whose summit I found to be infested with myriads of small flying ants (just like the Auvergne mountains in summer), are the remains of the celebrated labyrinth, one of the seven wonders of the world. Actually, hardly anything remains of it—just a few large slabs. What I found much more interesting was an enormous fossil vertebra, as thick as a fist, which I discovered in the loose earth of a canal which passes at that point. I do not know whether it will be possible to identify it.

Friday. We returned to Lahun, but this time by one of those little farm trains which run all over Fayoum, in order to spend the evening at the spot marked "farm" on my map. A former student lives there, leading a country life in a somewhat rococo

[1] Two bee-eaters were calmly devouring them. Bee-eaters are very plentiful now in Fayoum. [Note by Father Teilhard.]

house just on the outskirts of Fayoum. From his balcony, overlooking the fields and the desert, and facing the Pyramid of
Lahun, I observed with interest the scenes of farm life in Egypt.
In front of the house lay a great heap of some leguminous plant
which I had difficulty in recognizing. The grains were subsequently separated by a machine consisting of three series of
circular steel blades, topped by a seat, and harnessed to a
gamoosa. Gamoosas, bulls and donkeys were grazing berseem in
one area. Black wolfhounds were sleeping everywhere, awaiting
the night to howl.

The house, newly redone, was altogether typical of Coptic
taste. The outside was painted pink, the inside decorated with
crude frescoes representing a lady with a red umbrella (likeness
guaranteed) strolling at the edge of a lake on which swans
swim, or hunters sleeping on snowy ground while the game
dance around them, etc. The furnishings were all gimcrack—
pedestal tables, polished tables—and the floors were covered
with thick carpets, the lair of innumerable fleas. There were
six or seven of us in the drawing room: the master of the house,
in a green *galabieh* (robe) and embroidered cap, the village
omday, another Arab, a timber merchant, and a Coptic monk.
On a table, a phonograph (very typical, too, of Egyptian taste)
was playing Arabic airs. We met again at table to eat an
enormous silurus, prepared in our honor; the native guests were
chiefly interested in the bean patties and the herbs floating in a
clear sauce.

Saturday. Early in the morning we left for Enasia, situated
twelve miles south, at the level of the little town of Beni-Suef.
This contains the remains of a famous city, which my companion,
the archeologist, wished to visit. We made the trip on donkey-
back, over dams running across big wheat fields. From time to
time we passed through mud villages. Here, too, the countryside is too bare. The ruins of Enasia are considerable both in
extent and in the height of the mounds of debris. The remains

163

of a temple built by Ramses II were recently uncovered; it is nothing much, really.

Before we left, we had coffee at the village *omday's,* sitting on a carpet placed opposite the house. The return trip was trying; it was very hot, and our mounts were exhausted.

At the Lahun country house we found a completely authentic Coptic dinner. A big tray is covered with all sorts of small dishes (broiled fish, bean patties, onions, molasses, various herbs, indigestible pastries), and everyone takes what he wants with his fingers. Obviously, these people have no idea about nutrition; in any case, they eat very little.

Sunday. Rest. *Monday,* excursion to Kom Mushi, an old Greek city in the desert, to the north. You see that our excursions were weighted on the archeological side; the reason is that the good geological sites are very difficult of access, and desert trips require special preparation. If I return to Fayoum, I shall try to make better arrangements, now that I have had some experience of it.

The most curious sight of the day was the immense lands of Nubar Pasha near Tamieh. He bought 5,000 hectares for a song, which he improves and resells at a high price. It is large-scale agricultural enterprise, with small railroads, tractor plows, spreaders, managers on horseback, etc. The countryside as such is dreary: huge fields, absolutely treeless, abutting on yellow sands. Land improvements consists mainly in desalting and—which is far more difficult, apparently—denitrifying the soil. The land is drained and planted with rice, which absorbs the salt. We were received and shown around by one of the managers, an Armenian Catholic, who displayed touching affection for us.

The ruins of Kom Mushi are not particularly interesting. Little trains from the land development enterprise go there to collect the compost which fertilizes the fields, so we could be transported right to the site on a mule-drawn trolley. The debris of a small temple bear Greek inscriptions; one can see sections of earth walls and fragments of wooden bolts. The manager took us to his home to eat quail; he lives in a little earth farmhouse, quite comfortably, with his family. He is passionately fond of outdoor life, and seems to have plenty of drive.

Finally, yesterday, I got back safely, very pleased on the whole with my trip, which was very instructive. Tomorrow, classes begin again, and examinations take place in barely a month.

For some time I have been collecting a number of fine insects; I shall describe them to Biel in a letter I owe him. They include, in particular, two new buprestids.

Since I do not have much time today, and my letter is already long, I shall stop here. My thanks to Mother for her last letter; I think about her a lot. I do not know the Alexandria correspondent of *l'Univers*. But if he is an S.J., he has adopted a pseudonym.

Goodbye, dear Father and Mother, I kiss you and pray for you. My best to Guiguite and Joseph.[1]

Pierre

[1] The expedition described in this letter was the basis of an article published in *Relations d'Orient,* December 1907, 274–281: "Huit jours au Fayoum" "A Week at Fayoum"), by Pierre Teilhard de Chardin. This was Père Teilhard's first publication. The article concludes as follows: "All this, of course, is only the veneer. For the real results of this week on the shores of Lake Moeris, come and see the notes of the Egyptologist or my collections."

39

Dear Father and Mother,

So Toto has left now; I smiled when I learned about the size of the paper on which he wrote you his first letter, thereby conforming to the traditions of his brothers. I hope the poor youngster will soon find his feet.

Here there is little to report about the last two weeks; the most noteworthy fact is that we are nearing May 7, the date of the government examinations. The candidates are neither as numerous nor, especially, as brilliant as those of last year; but at least they will probably clear out and give their teachers some leisure. I am approaching my best time of the year.

Last week, we had two bouts of the khamsin, according to the book; a really hot wind (between 85 and 105 degrees), and frightful dust creating a fog. One bout started up on one of my days off, but I decided to go out just the same. At first it was hard, but after a while I got used to it, and we cleared away a full cubic yard of sand and clay without even thinking about the temperature. We were rewarded by digging up two vertebrae of a small fossil cetacean; one often comes across rib fragments, but rarely anything else.

Now the weather has changed, and we are going through a period of almost cold wind. This year, the weather really is as unpredictable as it could possibly be. With the lebbek acacias having just lost their last leaves and only beginning to grow their new ones, you would find the school yards looking much the same as the chestnut grove at this time. Fortunately spring is making good elsewhere; we have passed the perfumed season of the orange blossom; now the Barbary fig trees are putting on their lovely yellow flowers, and there is hardly a garden without the rich purple of the bougainvilleas.

To imitate Europe, we had a cab-driver strike. They were demanding some limit to the requirements of the society for the protection of animals; as soon as a shaweesh (policeman) notices a horse which he considers badly cared for, he takes the cab off to the police station (caracol), and the driver has to pay a large fine. Since the shaweesh receives a bonus for each arrest he makes, abuses certainly occur. Early in the year, the caracol was on our street for a time, and it was a curious sight indeed to see the jam of vehicles of every kind—trucks, cabs and even automobiles—which formed the rich loot of the police. The strike was well organized, without abstentions; the few who tried to operate were immediately surrounded, the traces cut and the cab overturned. Some twenty trams were damaged, so that in the end they moved only in groups of three, with shaweeshes in every car. One day, when the outlook appeared to be more menacing, the British even staged an imposing military parade; absolutely nothing moved. Now it is all over.

So Lord Cromer is leaving;[1] his successor has just arrived. His health, which is seriously impaired, appears to be the only reason for his departure, which everyone regrets, except, of course,

[1] After serving in Egypt for over twenty years, "His Excellency, Lord Cromer, Minister Plenipotentiary, Consul General and Diplomat Agent of England in Egypt," had just resigned, on April 11, 1907.

the Egyptian nationalist party. Though they will not be any the better off for it; the new man is still firmer, apparently, and that means hard.

Work on the "oases," or model garden cities, which big financiers are putting up in the desert north of Cairo, is going ahead actively. The general plan, it seems, is to create six between Cairo and Suez. For the time being, work is proceeding on two, the furthest off being some 7½ miles from Cairo. Huge sums are being invested; the first site includes an enormous hotel, a veritable palace of concrete which has already cost in the neighborhood of £60,000 to build. It will not open for at least another year, but it has already been decided to start work a month from now on an even larger hotel in the second oasis, complete with a small artificial lake for water sports (water-skiing). Apart from these huge constructions which are mush-rooming, there is not yet a single villa or a single inhabitant. The people responsible must certainly expect complete success, but many people regard it as rather a risky venture. Anyway, when it is ready, and when the big extra-fast packets begin their runs between Marseilles and Alexandria, there will no longer be any reason for Uncle Joseph not to spend a winter here.

Goodbye, dear Father and Mother, I kiss you as well as Guiguite, to whom I shall write next time.

Pierre

40

Dear Father and Mother,

I am not sure of the date of my last letter, but I have a feeling that I am late in writing. Fortunately this one will go by the Indian mail, which will save time. Anyway, this is the first time I am writing to you since May began, and I must tell you that I do not fail to pray to the Blessed Virgin, asking her to bless the family. This year you must have celebrated the feast of Notre Dame du Port on the smallest possible scale, but that is just one more reason for us to celebrate it even better. I am happy to learn that Toto is adjusting to Jersey, probably more quickly than you are accustoming yourselves to his absence; his first communion, I expect, will be on June 21. Here it takes place next Sunday. Last year, I was partly responsible for supervising the youngsters; this time, I merely have to give up a classroom adjoining the physics room to put up the retreatants, who are very numerous.

I told you last year how I felt about the first communion ceremonies here; they do not have the impressive quality of such ceremonies in France, because, it seems to me, the congregation does not really understand the importance of what is happening. This must be largely due to the contagion of the "orthodox," who are far from having the desired respect for the Blessed Sacrament. Still on the subject of ceremonies, last Thursday I had to speak to the students on the Ascension; it is an obligation which does not appeal to me, and I have little inclination to become an orator; but I have adopted the principle of never avoiding an opportunity to speak in public when it is offered to me. It is a necessary training, without which one is in danger of becoming altogether tongue-tied. As for last Thursday, I pulled it off satisfactorily.

The Egyptian baccalaureate examinations were taking place at the same time. As far as my subject is concerned, I think the candidates did fairly well; but who will ever know, especially here, where everyone is always triumphant, how good the papers really were? The results will not appear for at least ten days or so.

You will have read particulars concerning Cromer's departture in the papers. Throughout his term of office here, he insisted at ceremonies on observing his diplomatic rank after the agent of France; on the day he left, however, people apparently wanted to disguise nothing of the truth, and the farewells were those given to a sovereign. Two days earlier, he had made his famous speech at the Opera, which had been brilliantly decorated and surrounded by police; he had been more than ungracious to the khedive, who of course did not appear at any of the ceremonies. On the morning of his departure from Cairo, he slipped out by a roundabout route to his estates at Alexandria. Apparently the departure itself was very grand, with a line of soldiers drawn up from the palace to the station—that is, all the way through the European city.

I was not present, however, it being the famous Sham-el-Nessim (that is, perfume of the breeze), a kind of springtime feast, coinciding with the Orthodox and Coptic Easter Monday, at which the entire population, without distinction, rests or goes picnicking along the banks of the Nile. The students had the day off, of course, and I took advantage of it to go to the Lybian desert with three companions, plus a camel and a donkey. I am telling Guiguite about the insects I found there. It was hot, but there were still, here and there, many clumps of flowering trees. Out there, the rocks are chalky, white and jagged, and these ridges, often submerged in sand, bounding a wide, bare plateau where everything quivers and shimmers in the hot haze which rises from the ground, make a striking impression. What I noticed there especially was a nightjar (*Caprimulgus aegyptius*) which was almost crushed rather than abandon its nest, that is, two grey eggs laid in the sand. Shelley shows it against a verdant background, which seems to me inappropriate, and has the drawback of failing to emphasize the resemblance between the plumage and the color of the sand. If the one I saw had not run like a rat, I would not have noticed it. On the subject of birds, at Iñes Bey's I was able to identify a kind of wader, the size of a peewit, with reddish plumage, which abounds along the canals of Upper Egypt. It is the *Hoplopterus spinosus*. I was very surprised to see the quills it has on the tips of the wings.

As every year, sinister rumors circulated about a native uprising for Sham-el-Nessim, and of course nothing happened. It seems probable that Cromer left deliberately on that day to show his contempt for all such rumors.

I was almost forgetting to tell you that the epilogue of his departure for the school was the gift of some pious objects, of very high quality, which had belonged to his first wife, a Catholic, who died here; the gift was accompanied by a very tactful note.

Again, in the desert, I met a Bedouin, a camelherder, who was singular in that he was armed with an old Arab gun, more than two yards long, thin, with a small triangular butt, like the ones borne by all Horace Vernet's Arabs. It is the first of

171

its kind that I have seen here; usually the Arabs have old percussion or piston-rod guns.

Goodbye, dear Father and Mother, I kiss you as well as everyone at home, and I pray for you.

Pierre

41

Dear Father and Mother,

The photograph of Sarcenat in the midst of white meadows, which I received yesterday, gave me particular pleasure; apart from the charm of so many memories which it recalled, I was beginning to lose the notion of so lush a vegetation, and especially of one so varied. On another tack, I found the meeting between Yéyé and Mr. Delmas no less enjoyable; it was a long time since I had read any letters from Yéyé, and I was impressed by the development one can sense in him. If you knew what a difference that was from the young Cairo gentleman! And I could not help being touched by his zeal to pursue a Jesuit. By the way, have Biel and Yéyé tried to go to see Father Gras? He would enjoy them very much, and I think the reverse would also be true. Meanwhile, I suppose Mother is on her travels. I am happy for her at all the reunions, and I hope her stay at Jersey was agreeable. If I am not mistaken, it is the first time she has been present at the first communion of one of her sons. I hope she managed to cheer Gonzague up a bit. Incidentally, I readily agree with Father about him; he will go on being difficult as long as he remains at Bon Secours.

Now for the local news. First, the results of the examinations were deplorable: one out of five in philosophy, one out of about ten in the humanities. Apart from one failure which was a matter of bad luck, the philosophers got only what they deserved; of the humanists, four or five could have passed. Their consolation was in the curiously small proportion who passed in French, especially in relation to the number who passed in English. Of course, there was talk of injustice; perhaps it was simply a case of degrees of severity among examiners whose standards obviously were different. For the school, one thing is clear; the number of native students is very markedly declining in relation to the European element, and in such circumstances the Egyptian baccalaureate is less and less the desirable culmination of studies for the majority. Perhaps there will be changes next year.

Ten days ago, we celebrated Father Rector's birthday, according to ritual. Quite considerable gifts of macaroni, cigarettes, wine, rabbits, geese and sheep were made; then there was a dinner for the whole faculty, during which one took a wicked pleasure in noting the attitude of turbaned sheiks to their bottles. They all have very broad principles on the subject, and I saw some of them, at coffee, taking more liqueurs of their own accord. I find it very excusable, for if they had to follow all the prescriptions of the Koran, they could really hardly live a modern life. At least they put candy and sweetmeats above alcohol, as evidenced by my success when I passed around the fondants.

I took advantage of the holiday granted the following day to go on donkey-back to the big petrified forest. It resembles what one sees everywhere around here: slopes of dark red quartzite, strewn with silicified debris; some trunks are several yards long. We spent most of our time there catching grasshoppers, and Iñes Bey was delighted with some of the ones we caught. First, four specimens of a large type, noted only once at Mokattam, and remarkable by reason of its raised corselet in the form of a pointed galea. Then two specimens of a smaller type, with

174

red wings, which had not been observed before in Egypt, and which Iñes had come across at Sinai. But as you will see shortly, it seems to abound this year. For Father de Joannis, I collected a family of psyche caterpillars, which live in sheaths shaped like quadrangular pyramids and constructed with great artistry. They are at present all in their cocoons.

While we were eating on the side of a sun-baked slope, a Bedouin camelherder came to see us. We gave him some food (but he, for one, did not dare touch our water, for fear it might contain alcohol), after which he called us over to show us a big uromastix asleep near its hole. You probably know that the uromastix is an enormous lizard, with a big spiky tail, easily 32 to 36 inches long. The one we saw was a tremendous creature. The Bedouin came near it without awakening it, then suddenly lifted it by its tail, which is the most dangerous part. It struggled valiantly, but it was captive. We freed it, and it rushed off as fast as it could, throwing its legs out sideways, in very comical fashion. I think I told you that the Arabs hunt them to sell them to tourists as crocodiles. You often find them stuffed, sometimes at the doors of houses, to ward off the evil eye; but this was the first live one I had seen.

Last Sunday, that is to say, the day before yesterday, I spent the morning in the desert in the neighborhood of Helwan, together with Iñes Bey and a young man who is an ardent entomologist (he is the son of a powerful Greek, Shakur Pasha). We were after grasshoppers, and actually there were a lot of them; we found some more red ones, and two beautiful specimens, with purple wings, which Iñes did not have. It has not been classified yet. This year is certainly remarkable for its orthoptera and mylabrids; two of the types I was telling Guiguite about in my last letter were not in the Cairo collections; since then, we have all found several more specimens of them.

I do not know whether I told you about a small, all-black snake which a Fayoum farmer had given me; it turned out to be a young *Walterinnesia* type, of which there are only four known specimens (two in Cairo, one in London, one in Paris), all collected by Iñes. You see that one can find interesting things in these parts.

To round off the natural science chronicle, I have met a charming young man who is here to study Egyptian rocks. He is a pupil of Lacroix, at the Museum, an enthusiast, and full of latest ideas on petrology; he is going back to France for the vacation, where he will finish a doctoral thesis on the Normandy rocks which will take him to Jersey! How people's paths cross! If he can manage it, he will initiate me next year in the microscopic and chemical studies of rocks. Before he leaves, we shall go to visit the celestite deposits in the desert, which he has not yet seen, for lack of a guide. I am sorry not to have met him sooner.

Today is the opening of the season of prize essays; on the whole, this gives us more leisure. Friday, feast of the Sacred Heart, there will be a big procession, which worries me mainly on account of the altar boys; but the concern they give me will not prevent me from praying hard for you all on that day.

I kiss you.

Pierre

42

Dear Father and Mother,

All your letters have reached me very regularly. To answer everyone in turn, I shall begin by congratulating Guiguite on her scarab, and Biel on his photos; though a bit dark and less clear than "Sarcenat among the apple trees," they kindled old and very sweet memories for me, of times when I used to clamber about in the Puys too. The last time I went there with Albéric (on our return from Bayard, at Clermont), we went past the Puys of Gouttes and Chopine, right at the places shown in one of the photos. And now, Mother should not worry; a letter to Françoise went off four or five days ago; I was really shamefully late.

These past two weeks were mainly taken up with prize essays, and still more with correcting them. Now they are nearly over, and many of the students, persuaded that the same is true of the year, are beginning to take off for Europe with their families. A number, alas, cannot afford the luxury this time, in view of the lamentable state of finances in Cairo, where the exchange, after last year's wild speculations, is suffering a depression which is practically a disaster.

On the 21st, we renewed our vows, after the prescribed triduum, which obviously, in the midst of school life, can com-

177

mand only somewhat relative recollection. This did not stop me, as each time I give myself again to our Lord, from praying to him very specially for you, who have so great a part in the gift that I have been able to make him of myself. You know that I am as always perfectly happy in my life, and no less attached to my family.

In my last letter, I told you about my first encounters with my new acquaintance from the Museum, Mr. Couyat (from Bourbon); now we are a pair of friends, and I am sorry that he has to leave for Paris so soon; fortunately he will be back in October. Before he left, I went on two expeditions with him, to show him the celestite deposits at Mokattam which no one had shown him before (very few people in Cairo are interested in them, and the greater part of the year, if not all year 'round, I am the only one), and our search was successful. We brought back pounds of crystals, and since many types seemed to him new, he is going to publish a little note on them upon his arrival. Our investigations were disturbed only by the antics of our donkeys, which we had been foolish enough to bring without donkey drivers; hardly had we begun working than they began pulling on their halters, biting one another and tearing at their harnesses, or braying desperately. I did not think of tying stones to their tails. Actually I think the poor animals were terrified of the desert.

A letter from Mr. Pallary informed me that I had achieved a conchological success. Some quite insignificant little shells from the garden happen to be *Buliminus sennaaricus,* a type observed only in the regions of Abyssinia. In the entomological line, we gathered ample harvests of cocoons of egger and mimosa liparids; the caterpillars of the latter type (which fetches 25 francs) swarm on the little desert mimosas, but are quite difficult to breed because of the difficulty of finding food for them; they are lovely, incidentally, with carmine heads, golden yellow breasts, long hairs in white tufts, and very small. The *lasiocampa* [egger] is still more uncommon in collections, but here it is very readily to be found.

Incidentally, the name of the black snake I was telling you about in my last letter was definitely *Walterinnesia,* the reason being that Iñes Bey's first name is Walter.

Last Sunday, I had to supervise the outing of the altar boys, which consisted of taking them for a snack and a swim at Matariya—*"faire le bain"* ["make a bath"], as they say in their French. (The students here have a number of deplorable expressions; for instance, they will readily say: *"Je vous porterai mon père, etc."* ["I shall bring you my father . . ."] for *"J' amènerai . . .* ["I shall get him to come"].) The outing went off very well; anyway, as was only right, I had the cream of the school with me.

Goodbye, dear Father and Mother, I kiss you as well as Guiguite, Biel and Joseph. I was forgetting Yéyé, whom this letter will find at Sarcenat. Here our vacation begins on July 15.

Pierre

43

Dear Father and Mother,

This morning I gave my last class of the year, an event to which a teacher normally looks forward not without some pleasure; this evening, to wind things up, I am taking the science rhetoricians to look at the alternating current generators at the electricity works, and then the year will be really over. The only thing left is the French examinations to give in fourth; but that is not very hard, and my colleague will be my friend, Father Tissot, in whose company time cannot drag. Meanwhile, I enjoy a sudden popularity with those whom I am going to quiz tomorrow. They surround me with attentions—we are all alike. Prize-giving will be on Monday night, the 15th. Then there will be three quiet weeks, until about August 5, at which date we shall go to the seashore, at Alexandria, as last year.

The past two weeks have been very peaceful, and quite hot. I was nevertheless hero enough to climb the Mokattam hills, together with a Marist brother (there are some here for the lower grades), a native of the region around Ambert, and who is coming to be one of my best assistants in geology. We were lucky enough to unearth, from a sandy deposit, the finest cetacean vertebra I have yet found; I expect Mr. Fourtan will be filled with admiration for it. However, as the sand adhered to it very firmly, necessitating very careful cleaning, I decided to carry off a lump of rock almost as big as a man's head, the sight of which amazed quite a number of Cairo citizens whom I passed on my way home.

On the days when I make less distant outings, I follow the mud walls of Matariya to collect chrysalids for Mr. du Buysson; a consignment I sent him last year unfortunately went astray. This time I shall take more care.

All your letters have reached me regularly. I congratulate Orcines on getting a parish priest again. Father Garraud had told me that his brother had decided not to spend his vacation up there if there was no priest.

I want to thank Biel for sending me a view of the tree felling at Valettes; as he expected, it gave me great pleasure, and recalled many happy afternoons.

As regards the institute of the Sacred Heart, at Moulins, of whose alumni Xavier has the honor to be chairman, I do believe that my new friend from the Museum, Mr. Couyat, is a graduate; but I do not think he was present at the banquet.

Some time next week, I shall go to see Father Le Marois, who has the always coveted mission of escorting the Alexandria students to Cairo. He is right to take advantage of the opportunity; since he is going to Hastings in a few weeks, and does not belong to the Lyons province, he is not very likely to see the Orient again.

Does Joseph expect to pass a baccalaureate this year? From Mother's letters, I deduce that among various plans for next year he is thinking of Antoing. Without any prejudice in favor of the establishments of the order, I can only congratulate him on this; I have always heard Antoing spoken of as an excellent place for study, and I think it would be hard to find better

181

company than northerners, who are industrious and honest fellows.

As for me, everything thank God is still going very well in every way. I kiss you as well as the boys.

Pierre

44

Dear Father and Mother,

You will have received—with some astonishment, perhaps, on account of the French stamp—my letter announcing that Father Mulsant would be passing through Clermont. His departure was so hurried that I could not give him a longer letter. Anyway, he will be able to give you firsthand news of me, and bring me news of you.

I was agreeably surprised by the photograph of Françoise, which I was not expecting at all; I recognize her all right, and, with Guiguite, the only thing I have to find fault with is that her headband is too prominently displayed. I want to thank Mother for sending it to me so quickly. I was happy to see the boys, too, getting into the train at Gerzat; I do not find them changed. Only Gonzague's precious face is missing. Vialles, with its uncut hay, looked rather hirsute to me, but I admired the fountain. As for the view of Allier, I placed it at once, before reading Father's explanations.

So the vacation began two weeks ago. Prize-giving took place with the accustomed ceremony, and the attendance was even larger than usual. Mischief-makers explained this by the business setback in Cairo, which keeps many families far from Europe or Syria, where they usually escape at vacation time. Since then, I have been leading the most tranquil existence, between physics and natural history; in particular, I am preparing a remarkable consignment of butterflies for Father de Joannis.

Yesterday, I went to visit Iñes Bey at his laboratory in the

183

Medical School. I mention the fact because he was labeling a huge collection of Nile fish which had only just arrived. All the fish are in jars filled with alcohol; they lose some of their color there, but this is less important for the river types, with their dull colors, than for instance for the brilliantly colored types from the Red Sea. I admired the doctor's library at least as much as the fish; it gets the fascicles of practically all the important works on natural history in process of publication. In addition to books dealing especially with Africa, I noticed a complete description of lepidoptera throughout the world, all represented. Of course such a work can only be published in Germany. I also saw that Shelley is putting out a catalogue of African birds.

Next Monday, the 5th, we are leaving for Sidi Gaber, near Alexandria. It will be a change of scene, and it is always pleasant to see the sea again. I intend to scour the shores of Mariut as much as I can. You can write to me at Cairo as usual.

I close my letter on the feast of St. Ignatius, which in an empty school does not appear very impressive, of course. This does not prevent my praying to our Lord for you. In three weeks, at Hastings (the new residence of the "theologians"),[1] many of my good friends will be ordained priests, including H. du Passage.[2] Mother will be jealous—but my turn will come soon.

Goodbye, dear Father and Mother, I kiss you as well as Guiguite; I shall write to you without delay from Alexandria.

Pierre

[1] In 1902, while the scholasticate of philosophy of Laval emigrated to Jersey, the scholasticate of theology of Lyons-Fourvière moved to Canterbury. In the summer of 1907, it moved into the new building of Ore Place, on a hill overlooking the sea and the town of Hastings (Sussex). It was at Ore Place that Pierre Teilhard was to do his four years of theology, from 1908 to 1912. The scholasticate returned to Fourvière in 1926.

[2] Father Henri du Passage, of a family related to the Teilhards. For a long time he was director of *Études* in Paris.

45

Dear Father and Mother,

I could hardly believe my eyes when I read Guiguite's letter saying that she could walk. The improvement is certainly supernatural at least in that it came through the Blessed Virgin, and it is the best pledge of a complete cure, which I shall ask fervently with you of our Lady tomorrow, as I thank her. People are always telling of such more direct interventions of the goodness of the Blessed Virgin, but how much more moving they are when they concern one's own family. It is a proof that in heaven we are not forgotten, especially by those who have gone there—Albéric, Loulou.

After that, the news I can give you of myself seems very petty; here it is. First, I am writing to you from Sidi Gaber, on the very edge of the blue sea, which one never tires of watching, even though after a day or two one begins to long for the golden rocks of Cairo. Of course, we swim furiously in the warm water, and we breathe a deliciously fresh air.

In the last week I have hardly had time to be bored, thanks to my explorations around Lake Mariut. Twice I took a little train belonging to the khedive which leaves from a point west of Alexandria and crosses Mariut, then follows the southern edge of the lake for 50 miles, in the direction of Tripolitania.

185

I believe the line ends at the far end of the lake, at Abukir (you will find that on a good map), but I only went half way. In any case, the trip is very intriguing.

To the west of Alexandria, the desert starts immediately, and it consists of undulating rocky hills, dotted with the tents of Bedouin with very primitive manners and of bad repute (this does not exist in the Cairo desert, where one does not meet anyone). The train, incidentally, is almost exclusively used by the Bedouin. All along the line (at least along the stretch I covered), the activity of the khedive, who is the particular owner of all these lands, is displayed by attempts at cultivation. The stony soil is scratched by tiny swing-plows which the natives carry under their arms, and in spring the landscape must be quite green. At this point, fields cannot be distinguished. Here and there, near the stations, one sees the beginnings of sturdy plantations of dates, pomegranates and vines; they make a green splash in a desert which is grey as far as the eye can see. The whole problem is one of water.

My second trip, the furthest, was especially interesting. I bought a ticket at haphazard for a place called Behig, which turned out to be charming. In a long fold of land parallel to Mariut are several wells, and around them a little native center has formed; there is a large garden surrounded by rocks in which fig trees are crowded together, some low houses, and several hundred camels grazing the scanty grass around the "bir." To water the cattle, squads of half-naked natives draw water in a skin with a long cord, and pour it into little pools near which ungainly goats and camels gather impatiently. And all around, the desert. The Bedouins were very welcoming, and even the youngsters helped us to look for land shells, of which we harvested a magnificent collection. I shall write in more detail about them to Biel, but meanwhile I shall mention a fine helix with ornamental twirls which I had been asked for insistently, and which abounds in those parts.

I do not know if the maps still show in blue the long depression of Mariut which runs parallel to the sea. In point of fact, it is almost completely dried up as far as the point at which it connects with the big sheet of water which washes southern Alexandria. The fauna is not exactly similar to that of Cairo. I caught a very fine lizard, the size of a very large green lizard, with a yellow belly and an ash-grey back dotted with patches of bright orange. On a kind of small rosemary bush, I collected several psyche caterpillars with quadrangular sheaths, of the kind I had already found in Cairo. The desert is different from that at Cairo—less austere, and also less attractive. There were quantities of dried asphodel stalks; in spring the view must be delightful.

Yesterday, four of us, together with a young Alexandrian of our acquaintance, went for a sail in the roadstead. The port is very alive, with steamers, yachts and canoes from innumerable sailing clubs, and heavy Turkish sailboats with painted hulls, such as one sees in the illustrations of Jules Verne's *Archipel en feu;* and the wind was very pleasant.

Tomorrow we are going to the Alexandria school, where two priests are making their final vows.

Goodbye, dear Father and Mother, I kiss you as well as the family. I shall write you a few lines before my retreat. Once again, let us thank the Blessed Virgin and entrust the family even more to her care.

Pierre

46

Cairo, September 3, 1907

Dear Father and Mother,

I am very late in writing to you, but you will see from the detailed account of these three weeks that I have been quite busy.

The last days of vacation at Alexandria were very crowded. For instance, I spent a good day at Abukir at the villa of Edgar Shakur, a young and enthusiastic entomologist from Cairo. Abukir is a very beautiful seaside resort, with some villas and a whole camp of wattle huts to which Alexandrian families go to spend the summer. Such camps are very much in vogue. At Ras el-Barr, near the mouth of the Nile, at Damietta, there is a whole little straw town to which the best native families flock. The great attraction, apparently, is to cast off all the restraints of European life, and to be able to walk about barefoot and in a *galabieh* (Arab robe). In the way of military souvenirs, Abukir has a little fort and the Nelson islet. Naturally I concentrated mainly on insects, and we found a number of interesting specimens.

The distinctive feature of the terrain is the dune, bare or palm-covered. Immense estates are there, belonging to Prince Tussun, a cousin of the khedive, who himself owns the adjoining Montazah estates. Unfortunately the cousins have quarreled, and the khedive has succeeded in cutting off Prince Tussun's water, so that his lands remain of necessity absolutely uncultivated.

On another day, I toured the harbor in a very fine motor boat which a former student had recently brought back from Paris. We even had the boat blessed. Its maneuvers and its siren cause quite a stir; it is still practically the only boat of its kind at Alexandria. The former student in question had spent a month driving along the roads of Auvergne in an automobile; he had even been at Clermont for the review of July 14 (?).

Finally, on August 22, we went into retreat; despite his beard, which only makes him look even more austere, Father Dromard has not changed. A retreat, like most salutary things, is never much fun; but one feels the need for it if one is to do any good here. Naturally, I did not fail to pray for you and the family, and to give thanks again for Guiguite. Will you not be taking her to Lourdes, in thanksgiving, and to complete her cure?

I have just received Biel's letter, and Mother's, which makes me feel very guilty, since she says she is waiting for a letter. I am glad that satisfactory arrangements appear to have been made for a stay at Vialles, and congratulate Mr. Mayet on his unusual observations. If Father de Joannis happens to return to the area, Biel should try not to miss him.

I have also received a letter from Mr. Pallary, who tells me that, after almost being massacred at Casablanca, and again at Rabat, he was given shelter by le Gueydon. He still seems to be quite upset; his assignment was cut short forthwith. Two types of land shells which I had sent him at the beginning of August were unknown in North Africa.

To return to my activities of the past three weeks—as soon as I got back to Cairo I came upon a host of familiar faces; young priests from Beirut on their way to Hastings, or coming here, nearly all of whom I knew from Laval or Jersey. You can guess how busy they kept me, so great is the ambition to see the marvels of Cairo!

Then, on Sunday, Father Burdo arrived, and at that point I no longer had any time left at all. On Monday and Tuesday we made a big trip all the way past the first Pyramids. At the Giza Pyramids we hired two camels, which on the first evening took us to Saqqara, past the Abu-Sir group. Near Abu-Sir there is a temple which has recently been excavated. It is, apparently, of unique interest, because it is reminiscent of the Assyrian temples; a Pyramid stands in the midst of the enclosure (this never occurs in Egypt; the other Pyramids are tombs, flanked by temples to the east). Moreover, there remain a series of great alabaster troughs and long stones with trenches of unknown function. Nearby, the "sun ship," instead of being in bas-relief, or of wood, as elsewhere, is represented in raised brick: two walls following the same design. It is very strange. Some Germans are digging near another Pyramid, which provided us with the ever amusing scene of strings of children carrying baskets of turned-up soil on their head and singing in chorus. A worker had just been stung by a uraeus, which I could not see; he got over it with an injection.

We spent the night at Saqqara, in the earth house which Mariette had used. We slept rolled in blankets, lying on tables, under a veranda. I confess that I did not sleep too well, but it was a picturesque situation: camels grumbling at the door, Arabs saying their prayers, then lying down like ourselves; a donkey moving around in the midst of all this, munching beans. I heard some curlews singing (probably great plovers), which reminded me of nights in the Bravards.

The next day we continued south through the desert to the Dashur group, which few people visit. It consists of four Pyramids. The first measures 132 yards and is very regular; the second, much more curious, has its corners cut off (there was probably a change in plans in the process of building), and still has most of its smooth facing of large slabs. The charm of these Pyramids is that they stand in desert barely touched by excavation, and far from all civilization. The two others have almost completely collapsed. One, right on the edge of the Nile valley, is of black brick, like the ones at Fayoum; the last is nothing but a heap of rubble. Yet it was there that Mr. de Morgan found his famous queens' ornaments. His little house sheltered us for dinner. We had a delightful view there: the valley was completely flooded, as far as the Arabian desert, opposite; only the palms with their golden clusters stood out, with the earthen villages built on mounds.

The two days on camel-back had shaken us up considerably (Father Burdo photographed me on my mount, but he will not develop the film until he gets back to France), and we left them without much regret. A boat conveyed us over the flood waters to the train. It was a trip which I shall remember with great pleasure.

Most of our visitors are leaving us tomorrow. There have been many changes in the personnel of the school, but a lot of us are old acquaintances nevertheless. My basic duties remain unchanged; as for details, they have not yet been determined, but they will be soon, as Father Mulsant returned yesterday—without having been to Clermont.

I shall write to you again without too much delay. Meanwhile, I kiss you with all my heart, as well as Guiguite and the boys.

Pierre

My best wishes to Uncle Joseph, and to the inhabitants of the Bravards.

191

47

Dear Father and Mother,

We are getting quite near the beginning of term, which here is on October 2, and it will not be long for the boys either, alas. Poor Joseph's departure will create quite a void for you, as he had got you out of the habit of his absence. Will Father go as far as Brussels, or some other Belgian city?

My duties are little changed this year. In addition to the upper classes, I am going to take the third for physics again (as in my first year); on the other hand, I am relieved of the—not very heavy—responsibility for the altar boys. I expect I shall go on riding into town daily to pick up the young children in the bus, but that is more of an entertainment than anything else. One thing is still not settled, namely the composition and distribution of classes (that is, the timetable), which is more important for the teachers than one might imagine. However, in this country it is impossible to know before school opens whether a particular student wishes to take letters or science.

Pending October 2, I get around Cairo quite a bit, with varying degrees of success. Last week, I spent a day in the Turah mountains (they are slightly south of Cairo, between Cairo and Helwan), a much finer region than Mokattam. We went quite far up a very beautiful wadi, a real river bed, some one hundred and fifty yards wide, embanked between two cliffs. The vegetation at the bottom of the wadi is relatively abundant; that is, in addition to the clumps of graminaceae or zygophyllum, there are little shrubs here and there with pretty purple flowers. In the spring, the place must be delightful, and rich in insect life. Last week there were only some large green scorpions and some black crows with brown heads (*Corvus umbrinus*). In the debris piled up by the winter rains, I collected a good many specimens of a small shell (*Chondrus* ...) which so far, I believe, has been found only in the high mountains in the vicinity of the Red Sea. We had taken along a little Arab to look after our donkeys; he was terrified when he saw us going so far, and sobbed his heart out, and we had very great difficulty in making him come all the way.

At Mokattam, we caught a little "viper of the pyramids" (*Echis carinata*). It was the first I had seen, though I understand that it is very common. When it feels itself in danger, it rubs the folds of its body together, making a noise that sounds like "ay," very loud and very distinctive.

Yesterday, I went bug-hunting in the direction of Helwan with Dr. Iñes Bey. We collected mostly orthoptera, grasshoppers with purple wings, and an interesting type of heremiophilids. The latter look something like the sketch below; they are a kind of mantis with rudimentary wings and huge feet, and they run like the wind on the sand, with which their color blends completely. It is a type of insect which really belongs to the desert, and is very interesting.

Mr. Robert de Buysson wrote to me about some chrysalids which I had sent him. There were more types than I had thought, and in two cases I was lucky enough to have caught mostly males, when only the female was known, and vice versa. This encourages me to continue.

Yesterday I heard a rather amusing story about a young Syrian Father who had never left the East, and who three weeks

193

ago found himself transplanted to Chatel Guyon for a season.
The first time he went out of the hotel, he saw some good ladies
in bonnets. Taking them for nuns, he began speaking to them,
and addressed them as "Sister . . ." Apparently his mistake was
taken in quite good part.

Goodbye, dear Father and Mother, I kiss you as well as
Guiguite and the boys. I shall think of you especially on the 27th;
Albéric will obtain for us that this year should be a good one for
your older children.

Pierre

Has Françoise told you of the death of Father de Verneuil's
sister, her "good mother" of La Tour?

Congratulations to Yéyé on his pheasant.

I would like Joseph to send me his address at Antoing.

48

Dear Father and Mother,

My last letter left some hours before yours arrived telling me about the crisis which had arisen concerning Gonzague's future. I am very happy about the way it has been resolved, but it would be good if the little fellow really decided to work. Judging by the descriptions I have been given of Marneffe, he and Toto are going to find a lush countryside there, which will compensate them somewhat for the absence of the sea. I suppose Father de Vallois is still rector; I knew him for a year at Jersey, and he is one of the most charming men I have ever met. As for the faculty, it consists mostly of young men who did their philosophy with me. The absence of all these boys, including Joseph now, must make the house very empty. In return for the sorrow this causes you, our Lord will surely bless their year.

Here, school has opened again, and rarely has such a full complement been seen on the first day; usually returns are staggered over the whole of the month, and beyond. But this year, there is still a business crisis which has reduced the price of land, and prevents many people from traveling. In Cairo, and even more in Alexandria, many families are in very difficult circumstances.

I do not start my classes until tomorrow, and my only

complaint is that my schedule is fairly complicated, given the great number of students I am dealing with. So far, I have only had to worry about getting the young new boys home; they either have only vague ideas as to where they live, or know too little French to explain. In that connection, what Mr. Jacquemont told Mother about my Arabic studies is unfortunately only an ideal; I have hardly any time for them, and very few opportunities. I regret it sorely; Arabs are very happy when one talks to them, and apart from the very useful information one can get from them, they welcome it when one chats with them about moral, and even religious truths.

To close the vacation, I spent a day at Abu-Roach, in the desert north of the Pyramids. I brought back some sea-urchins which may be interesting, and some celestite crystals which will delight Mr. Couyat.

Let me inform you that the latter has reported to the Academy of Sciences on the ones we collected in June at Mokattam; but I have seen only the notice of the report, which I shall probably soon receive *in extenso*.

Goodbye, dear Father and Mother, I kiss you and pray for you. All good things to Biel; I want to write to him fairly soon.

Pierre

49

Dear Father and Mother,

I have received all your latest letters regularly, full of details of the boys' return to school. I was very interested in Father's account of his trip to Belgium, though not surprised at what he said about Antoing and Marneffe. It falls to Gonzague and Toto to experience a type of school life whose advantages they probably do not fully realize, nor its superiority over that which their seniors had to endure—at least as regards amenities. I shall write to that rascal, Gonzague (this is for Mother), who happens to be in the class of one of my best friends, who will really be able to make him work seriously.

I think you have taken the best decision for Guiguite, and we must hope that the Blessed Virgin will be pleased. I pray hard with you.

The days here pass with lightning speed, faster than in vacation time, I find, but also more uniformly. My two large lower classes (humanities and third), concerning which I had felt some apprehension, are on the contrary giving me great satisfaction; they include a clear majority of really nice youngsters, who listen to me with admirable attention. Unfortunately, I cannot yet give them anything very interesting to do. On the other hand, my rhetoric-science class is not as good as last year's. Personally,

I am, as is only right, in much better control of my teaching, and am beginning to taste the joy of teaching something to others, which in my case is much less than the joy I derive from learning something for myself. May our Lord also have me do some good to all these youngsters.

Since school opened, I have managed to make a couple of trips. Yesterday, in particular, thanks to the new boys' holiday, I went on donkey-back all day through the undulating and pebbly northeastern desert, along the ancient route of the Indian mail. The very distinctive vegetation of this part of the desert consists mostly of big clumps of graminaceae with hard and spiky leaves, growing here and there. It was in such clumps, though not so far away, that a week ago I collected a kind of pale yellow grasshopper, rather like a cricket, which Iñes Bey was delighted with, and which has not yet been classified. I did not find any more yesterday, and the main interest of the trip was geological; I was able to hammer some basalt, which was in quite poor condition, and some Miocene deposits, which were interesting, though poor in fossils. A pretty fox darted off under my feet. I came across a new desert bird which I did not know, but to which Brehm may refer; it is a kind of lark, *Certhilauda desertorum,* with black and white wings, which I had mistaken at first for a wader, but which Iñes Bey, who was with me at the time, identified for me.

Christian Burdo has sent me, for you, my picture on camel-back; if Mother still wants to be reassured concerning my appearance, she should remember that the sun was shining right into my face, and that we had been riding camels for two days, without any previous experience. Behind the animal which I was riding you can see the Pyramid of Dashur, with its cut corners.

By way of local news—Ramadan has started; the mosques are lit up, the native children run about the streets with little lanterns, and the government offices operate on a modified schedule on account of the fast.

Goodbye, dear Father and Mother, I kiss you as well as Guiguite and Biel.

Pierre

P.S. I am reading a book in which, as an example of graphs of train schedules, the author has selected the Clermont-Laqueuille line. I recognize all the times . . .

50

Dear Father and Mother,

When this letter arrives at Sarcenat, Mother will probably be in Lourdes with Guiguite; whatever the outcome of the journey, we shall not have been represented at the grotto in vain, and they will certainly return with many blessings from our Lady. Mother will have found memories of her last visit, and perhaps even the venerable landladies for whose furnishings Yéyé used to make her tremble. I, too, am happy to think that she is seeing all those places again.

Tomorrow, as every year, I shall be very much united with you in praying to the saints of the family; we may be sure that they do not forget us and protect those who remain. You know that I like to tell you again, on those days, how attached I remain to you, regardless of time and distance. I believe it is truer every year.

Here the regular routine continues; the first month is over, which for me means that a program has been seriously tackled. Tomorrow the last group of latecomers will probably turn up; this time, they will not have escaped the retreat, which exceptionally is not taking place until next week, just at the time of the big celebrations for the close of Ramadan. The coincidence is really very fortunate; the Moslems can be sent to celebrate in their homes without disrupting the classes, and without extra holidays.

Iñes Bey has established the practice of inviting me "hunting" every Sunday; as he is a charming man, who teaches me many things, there is nothing disagreeable about this, though in general my explorations are more fruitful when I go out alone. Often he is accompanied by one of his acquaintances, so that I make contact with some very pleasant persons. For the past two Sundays he has been acting as guide to the young son of one of his friends (Dr. Fouquet, a great lover of Arab art), a budding entomologist, who told me with enthusiasm how he had caught an *Apatura iris* in Dauphiné in August. Except that he shrinks from touching cow-dung and caterpillars, to which I am trying to harden him, he gives me a good picture of what we must have been like when we began "collecting." He is furthermore a young Frenchman with perfect manners. I supplied him with some local curiosities, which he will probably not prize at their true worth. On the subject of overcoming aversions, I have heard about an enthusiastic collector of insects here who has just got married and is teaching his wife to catch cockroaches with her hands; certainly an odd fellow.

Mr. du Buysson has written to me to say that he is going to send me, by Mr. Couyat, his book on chrysalids, a work of considerable dimensions; he asks me also to collect gadflies and other stinging Diptera for him, as they are being studied a great deal now in connection with the transmission of diseases. I have the impression that the species are not very abundant here. Possibly more detailed investigation will cause me to change my mind on this score.

A week ago we had a very violent storm; that is how the summer usually ends. The clouds banked up in the evening, moving up the Nile, and from our terrace the sight was remarkable:

201

half the sky was black, all fissured with such beautiful flashes that I had my science students leave their work to show them this display of electricity; the other half, above the desert, was without a vapor, and the full moon was rising. The storm began with an avalanche of hailstones, many of which were as big as nuts; then there was a little rain; and fifteen minutes later, the sky was studded with stars. What was most typical was the joy of the Arabs, who all ran into the streets to pick up the hailstones and eat them. Since then, we have had a couple of hot days, with temperatures up to about 85 degrees.

I hope, for Biel's sake, that snow has come to Auvergne, with the woodcocks.

Goodbye, dear Father and Mother, I kiss you with all my heart.

Pierre

What a delightful son you have in your dear Pierre, in whom I find much of *our* dear Albéric! Albéric was one of those whom heaven does not like to leave long on earth. Bless God, our Lord, for having given you such good children. How I bless him for the graces given to your daughter! I want you to know that I am very happy indeed to be able to try to take your place at the side of this dear Pierre whose Father I, too, have the joy to be.

Sincerely yours in the Heart of our Lord,

A. André, S.J.

51

Cairo, November 22, [1907]

Dear Father and Mother,

I received Mother's letter yesterday, from Lourdes. From our point of view, the result of the trip is a little disappointing, but obviously we can only leave it to the Blessed Virgin to do as she thinks fit; she will effect a cure in her own good time, and meanwhile you are sure to have done everything in your power. In spite of everything, Guiguite must have enjoyed her stay there.

You must find that I am quite behind in writing to you. One of the reasons for this delay is that the day before yesterday I had to give some physics tests at Alexandria, just as the teacher at Alexandria is to come here in a week's time to quiz my students. It is a new system, which makes the students work harder, and promises me more than one appearance on the Mediterranean shore. The journey was very agreeable, and called up many pleasant vacation memories. Good trains make the trip (131 miles) in three hours, so that I was absent for only twenty-four hours. I had time to see many friends there again; and it is always amusing to see a school in operation which is not one's own, and where one has no responsibilities.

The Alexandria school is much more like a French school than ours; the programs are conventional, and the students for the most part belong to European families. There are some fine boys among them, but it is terribly worldly, like society there. I think I was merciful to my candidates, who were sufficiently few in number for me to be able to get them to talk at some length, and interestingly.

Yesterday afternoon I went to Sidi Gaber, where I saw the waves break much more vigorously than in August. The weather was bad; squalls were blowing up, and the water was an unpleasant greenish color, right for the Jersey coasts.

I came back here with a supply of dead leaves from the garden at Alexandria which I intend to examine at leisure for small types of shells. So far I have found only one. That is not much.

I traveled with a Senegalese who was at pains to talk to me in very correct French, and with all the warmth of a compatriot; natives of British colonies would certainly not talk like that with nationals of the mother country.

Did you read, in the *Correspondant* of October 10, I believe, an article by C. Hearty entitled "Reminiscences," or "Impressions of Army Life"? It was by Father de Bélinay, doing his final twenty-eight days; it was his goodbye to his regiment. The reason I mention it now is that only yesterday did I have occasion to read it.

Mother will be pleased to hear that Father Lenoir, Gonzague's teacher, has told me in a letter that Gonzague is beginning to blossom out; I know Father Lenoir[1] well, and I think Gonzague could hardly have found anyone better.

You may know from the papers that Mr. Aulard has made a new inspection of the schools of the east. This time all the school saw was his visiting card, and he had the tact not to ask to visit the classes. He is leaving for France today.

Last week, the khedive returned to Cairo, which will help to enliven the city, together with the tourists, who are beginning to arrive. Yesterday, as I left the train, I was astonished at the

---

[1] Father Louis Lenoir (1879–1917). See Georges Guitton, *Un "preneur d'âmes," Louis Lenoir, s.j., aumônier des Marsouins*, 1914–1917, Paris 1922.

press of buses and splendid cars which canvass the wealthy traveler in order to take him off to exorbitantly priced hotels.

Last Thursday, I conscientiously watched Mercury pass across the sun; I expect Biel will have done the same with the telescope at Sarcenat. Incidentally, congratulations to him on his woodcocks.

Goodbye, dear Father and Mother, I kiss you, as well as Biel, and I pray for you.

Pierre

52

Dear Father and Mother,

This letter will reach you just at the time Gabriel leaves, and that, coupled with poor Guiguite's enforced inaction again, is not calculated to brighten the atmosphere. Fortunately Christmas is not far off, and then we have to reflect that our Lord will take account of all these sacrifices to bless the family in the manner he pleases. I shall not fail to pray hard for you all on the 8th, that is, the day after tomorrow.

On Sunday a week, the school will go to Matariya in a body for the annual procession; it will seem strange not to have to supervise the altar boys for the occasion. Perhaps I shall appreciate the ceremony the more for that, but I am not sure; there is nothing like organizing something for discovering all kinds of hidden beauty in it. Anyway, the Nile countryside now provides one of the most beautiful and most peaceful settings that one could dream of: the fields are verdant with clover (*birsim*) and beans; the mimosas have all their leaves owing to the flooding of the Nile; and on all this the light falls much more softly, though just as brightly. The gardens, moreover, like the one at Matariya, have the added attraction of many orange and tangerine trees. But usually a foreseeing hand passes there before the procession to avoid leading the students into temptation.

Mr. Couyat has returned to Cairo, but for the moment he is very taken up with the problems of moving, as the French Institute is changing its penates. So far I have seen him properly only once. He brought me, from Mr. du Buysson, a voluminous and profound work on chrysalids, with certain species classified thanks to specimens which I had sent him.

To complete the roll of my correspondents, a certain Mr. Prieur, of Paris, to whom I had sent all my finds of fish teeth, informed me that he had presented a note on these finds to the Geological Society of France. There is a new species and three new varieties, one of which is a *Teilhardi* (!). I shall send you the memorandum, as a curiosity, as soon as I receive copies of it, that is, in two or three months' time.

Last Monday, as usual, I attended the monthly meeting of the Egyptian Institute, which is interesting chiefly because one meets friends or persons of note. I had the privilege of hearing the honorary chairman, Mr. Maspero,[1] speak, roundly challenging the somewhat absurd contentions of a lecturer. Physically, he is a little man with a small white beard, and with the classical features of a distinguished university man; it is really music to hear him speak. The transition was all the more painful when a pasha followed him in his halting speech. In theory, the Institute is the continuation of the one founded by Bonaparte. In fact, it is still very French in composition; only since last year have lectures in English been permitted—which anyway is a bad omen. The English will not be satisfied with this concession, and the establishment may one day, alas, be Anglicized for good.

There is no school news, except that a courtyard is being asphalted, to the delight of the little boys, who immediately proceeded to skate all over it. That reminds me to tell you that the diabolo craze is beginning to catch on here, a year or two after Europe, as is only proper. However, what are displayed

[1] Gaston Maspero, the famous Egyptologist.

207

here at the same time as in Paris are the Printemps[2] and Louvre[2] toys, at their branches here. The natives line up to look at the mechanical puppets.

Goodbye, dear Father and Mother, I kiss you, and love you always with all my heart.

Pierre

[2] French department stores—tr.

53

My Dear Father,

This year, on Christmas Eve, you will miss the stories, and the stockings too; it will be the first time in a long while, and you will certainly feel it. But after all, in spite of the varying degrees of distance which separate us from you, the fact remains that your children love you much more deeply and more consciously, and that is the compensation. No one will forget you on the 25th, and for my part I am writing to you as usual to wish you a happy holiday. I ask our Lord to bless you and, if he wishes, to make this year a happier one than the years before. Basically, it is perhaps those which will mean most to us.

Now for some news about life in Cairo during the past two weeks.

First, one of Egypt's visitors has been—and perhaps still is— your very honorable and illustrious colleague, Maurice Barrès,[1] who arrived here in the company of a number of journalists to christen the *Heliopolis*. The *Heliopolis* and the *Cairo* are two magnificent turbine steamers, which travel at 22 knots (almost as fast as the transatlantic boats), which a powerful Anglo-Egyptian

[1] Maurice Barrès belonged to the Academy of Sciences, Belles-Lettres and Arts of Clermont Ferrand, of which Emmanuel Teilhard de Chardin was permanent secretary.

concern has just put into service to do the run from Marseilles to Alexandria in three days and some hours. The first trip was successful, and was celebrated by a number of festivities in the European colony.

Today, it is the Moslem element which is rejoicing over the departure of the sacred carpet which Cairo sends each year to Mecca (Damascus does the same). A French gentleman, Boniteau Bey, who supervises the organization at the ministry, gave me some interesting particulars on the subject. This year, 1,800 pilgrims are joining the official caravan in order to enjoy the protection of the armed escort which accompanies the carpet. All these people embark at Suez, and disembark at Jidda, and this crowd, mounted on some 2,000 camels, reaches Mecca in one day. The Arabs there are given a very large sum so that they shall respect the pilgrims and not rob them. This money was stolen some years ago aboard the train between Cairo and Suez! Formerly, pilgrims went to Suez on foot; they assembled near Matariya and, taking a short cut through the desert, quickly reached the Red Sea.

Last Thursday, with a few students, I visited a spot—or a hole, rather—of Cairo which I did not know: Joseph's well (no connection with the patriarch; the Joseph here was Yusuf Salah el-Din, that is, Saladin himself). It is a rectangular well, dug right in the rock at the summit of the Citadel, and descending to the level of the Nile. One descends the first part, which is close on 130 yards deep, by a spiral path, dug in the rock wall, along which oxen could move to turn the sakieh (wheel which turns a series of jars) whereby water was raised from the lower floor. This second floor is almost completely closed, but the stones one throws in take a considerable time to reach the bottom. A second sakieh, set up at the very top, was to pick up the water brought up half-way by the first.

Last Sunday we had the procession at Matariya which I had

mentioned to you. Everything went off very well. The special train which took the students and guests was impressive.

Goodbye, dear Father, I kiss you as well as Mother and Guiguite. Again, a happy holiday.

Pierre

54

Cairo, December 29, 1907

Dear Father and Mother,

I realize to my sorrow that, as usual, I have again fallen
behind; yet I would so much have liked this letter to arrive at a
time when you were all together, so that I could wish you all a
happy new year as a body. As I said a week ago in my letter to
Father, you know how attached I remain to you. I do my best to
ask our Lord, for whom I left you, to bless the coming months
for you according to his will. He will surely make them serve
to bring us closer to him. In case the Marneffe people are still at
Clermont, I want to wish them especially a happy new year; they
are the ones whom I have left longest without news.

This time I shall not go to Luxor, but only to Minya, during
the vacation. It is less romantic, but also less well known from
a geological point of view, and I hope to reap a good harvest.
In any case, I am very pleased about this new trip to Upper
Egypt, which is lovely country. Also, we shall be three "youngsters" together, which promises a good time. Tomorrow, to close
the year, there is to be a little performance, in the form of a
pastorale. I have just come back from a rehearsal (but don't
imagine that I am one of the organizers), and it should be quite
pretty. In particular, there is a little Jesus (a pupil in ninth) who
sucks his thumb with consummate sincerity; the gesture is natural

to him. Father Mulsant, who is a first-rate organizer and designer, especially arranged the sets in pure Egyptian style (one "tableau" takes place in Egypt, with Joseph), with an abundance of lotuses and vultures.

The feast of Christmas went off very well, as did midnight Mass—as well as it could when it is not cold, and there is no chance of snow.

I want to thank Joseph for his letter. Fortunately, there was a priest here from Champagne who could help me decipher the name of his teacher; to the latter I have sent particulars concerning Jersey, and promised some specimens from Egypt. I confess that my desire to win Father Curmien's good graces for Joseph had some part in my decision.

It is said that the Empress Eugenie is coming here this winter; she paid a visit here four years ago. Yet it must be singularly bitter for her to come as a tourist to a city where a former khedive spent the earth to receive her, and where her former palace has become a big hotel (Gezineh Palace). As regards tourists, so far they appear to be conspicuous by their absence; the Americans, especially, leave a big vacuum, for it is not their year for traveling.

I have no doubt that the people at the rue du Port triumphantly showed Mother my little relation on Fayoum, in *Lettres d'Orient*. It will not have taught you anything. On the other hand, the preceding pages, by Father Tissot, will give you more information about Cairo.

Goodbye, dear Father and Mother, I kiss you. Next time, I shall probably write to you at rather great length. I want to thank Mother for her last letter, which gave me much pleasure. I still have no news about my buprestid (that is for Guiguite). Again, a happy new year.

Pierre

213

55

Dear Father and Mother,

As you see from the letterhead, I have got further into Upper Egypt than I had hoped three days ago. A little Copt whom I had to accompany here was the occasion of this windfall, and it really is one. I left yesterday *morning* at 8:30, and was to arrive here, in theory, at midnight. Actually I arrived at 1:30 a.m., so that I spent from 1907 to 1908 in the Kena station. I thought of you at the time, and I prayed for the family. I also remembered that Kena is the place from which caravans leave to go to Qosseir, on the Red Sea, relatively close to here. You know, perhaps, that Desaix made that trip, and I would gladly have imitated him, at least in order to see the emeralds of the Jebel Zabara.

Some find the journey from Cairo to Luxor tedious; for me, the eighteen hours passed quite quickly, and just the feeling that one was traveling south was in itself deeply satisfying. But, in addition, the countryside is really ideal, with its very special character of quiet in bright light. The physical features are those of the region immediately south of Cairo, but more and more accentuated; sometimes the cultivated belt narrows still more, and the desert bounds it with increasingly high cliffs. One passes the great desert plateaux, now of the Arabian chain, now of the Libyan chain, and my impressions of the journey will eventually merge in a picture of the high wall, pink in the morning, white at noon, pearly at night in the full moon (as it was when I saw it), bordered by the Nile or by a sea of flowering beans whose perfume filled the train.

There are no big towns on the way, only some small places like Beni Suef, Minya or Assiut, the latter miming Cairo a little with its minarets and the high promontory jutting out above it. I believe it is very densely populated, but the people are probably shut in in the mud villages one sees at long intervals, for the fields stretch on as far as the eye can see, without a habitation. Moreover, these are a special kind of fields; from Minya on, where the jungles of sugar cane seemed to me to thin out, all you see are continuous stretches of dark green, where clover (berseem: *Trifolium alexandrinum*) and the aforementioned beans succeed one another with transition. Judging by the thickness of all these forages, the fertility of the Nile mud is no myth. I forgot to mention the big fields of onions; they are typical.

I think one can see some antiquities from the train, but they would be in the section which I saw by moonlight, which is beautiful for showing up the palm trees and their silvery reflections, but otherwise insufficient.

The population, too, clearly becomes more and more indigenous; from Cairo on, one sees almost only tarbooshes and turbans, and then the turbans predominate. Around Minya, there are a number of Coptic villages, Catholic or Orthodox according to the pastor. Here I was struck by the beauty of type of the inhabitants. With their fine copper-colored skin and their big white turbans, they preserve exactly the type of the Egyptian statues—thickish lips and nose, but a proud and remarkably intelligent cast of features.

Luxor is a small, very indigenous town, with an annex of small hotels, American Bible societies, etc. This morning at 8 o'clock I was on the banks of the Nile; a profusion of boats with large triangular sails were unloading stones, eggs, herbs, in a setting of palms and Arab houses, and, furthermore, against an indescribable horizon: beyond the Nile, a green belt, and a mile or so beyond that, the Libyan wall, very high and precipitous, and all pink, with a slight bluish haze around the foothills. Here, light is everything.

I have just come back from visiting Karnak. Memphis is nothing compared with this enclosure with its accumulation of great pylons, obelisks, and great lotus-shaped columns (flower or bud). This is where the bulk of the restoration work is going on, directed by a Frenchman, Mr. Legrain. Everything is covered with large inscriptions and bas-reliefs, showing in particular different Ramses offering various gifts to the god Amon. An avenue of sphinxes with rams' head, more or less dilapidated, leads up to each of the temples. The avenue leading from the great temple used to extend as far as the foot of the mountains, two miles away, on the other side of the Nile. In those days, the Nile did not flow where it does now. Its bed has shifted somewhat, like the Allier's. The obelisk at the Concorde[1] comes from the great temple. In its enclosure there are two sacred lakes where a symbolic boat used to float; I noticed two wild ducks there living in great security.

I am continuing my letter this evening. At noon I went to visit the temple at Luxor. It is similar to the great temple of Karnak, but does not have its setting of palms. It is separated from the Nile by a quay, and a part of it has disappeared under a rubbish heap topped by a mosque. It is quite common for Arab villages gradually to rise on the heaps of rubbish which collect around them. Since the area of the mosque is by its very nature sacred, there is no knowing when excavations can begin there. One of the principal Cairo streets bends sharply in deference to the tomb of a saint (a hovel where a beggar used to live who was regarded as a saint)!

[1] The Place de la Concorde, in Paris—tr.

Nevertheless, what remains and what has been restored is tremendous; particularly the colossi of Ramses, standing, carved in monoliths of rose granite. Only two faces have been preserved, but the expressions are very fine. Unfortunately, the walls and columns were built of the famous Nubian sandstone, which crumbles terribly. I say famous, because its great quarries are well known, in the Jebel Silsileh, above Aswan (to the north), and especially because it is one of the most important and most disputed areas of Africa. A part of the temple is very well preserved; it is a small sanctuary built by Alexander the Great, where he himself is featured as Pharaoh! It is a strange sensation to find these traces of so classic a hero, but the place is not as venerable as Memphis.

As I left, I entertained myself going past the displays of "antiquities." Arabs spread towels in front of them on which they place necklaces, small statues, tamarisk beetles (a little Arab offered me one this morning which was struggling, pierced by an enormous nail) and, especially, the inevitable scarab, as big as a hand or as small as a nail, green, amethyst, of every shape; there is a native factory not far from here where they are manufactured, and the tourists delight in them.

Tourists are quite plentiful now, and this morning I realized the truth of the statement that Cook is the true master of Egypt; I saw sixty English and American tourists, followed by an army of donkey drivers and preceded by a dragoman, invade Karnak; in front of each temple, they would stop and the dragoman would given them an instruction; then they would look around and go out. I had dinner in sight of a table of about ten young American ladies; it was quite entertaining.

To round off the day, I returned to see Karnak in the evening and went back in a dazzling sunset. A big fan of clouds, finely striated and diaphanous, suddenly seemed to catch fire, and for fifteen minutes it was a veritable dome turning gradually from pale gold to dark red; the Nile, of course, was doing the same, and the big boats filled with white turbans were slowly transformed into Chinese shadows.

I was forgetting to tell you that I shall be here until the day after tomorrow, at which time I am going on to Minya. The father of the young student who brought me here, a (native) French consul and fabulously wealthy, who is at present in Cairo, instructed his secretary to see to it that I received every consideration. Three times, at least, the secretary has come with great ceremony to make sure that I lacked nothing. Since he knows only Arabic, we use the services of an interpreter, who faithfully transmits to me his wishes for health and prosperity.

January 3. I have just returned from the traditional excursion to the Royal Tombs. At Thebes, as at Memphis, the cities of the dead were in the desert, but here, instead of the meagre cliff of Saqqara, you find beautiful rugged mountains. The funeral chambers were dug at the entrance to a valley, at the bottom of a deep amphitheatre. So far, thirty-five tombs have been found, the last one five years ago. One enters them by means of long passages and stairs, which are lit, like the chambers, by electricity. The paintings are marvelously preserved, and more magnificent in style than those at Saqqara. Here one no longer sees lines of servants bringing gifts; the defunct king is pictured together with sundry divinities, or there are scenes of funerals where sacred ships and a huge sacred serpent play a great part. Sculptured and painted serpents guard the entrance to the doors. At the site of the corridors, one inevitably finds a big scarab and a crocodile. These are the tombs in which most of the royal mummies have been found, and, in the last one, a whole sacred ship, which is now in Cairo.

To reach the place, I crossed the Nile at 8 a.m. in a boat belonging to the consul; on the other side, sturdy donkeys were waiting, which carried me through the verdant fields to the desert. I saw many bee-eaters, and swarms of pigeons; they nest in big dove-cots of unbaked clay consisting of a tower topped by something like pitchers the wrong way up, which serve as nests. Incidentally, the natives fashion the Nile clay into very unexpected objects. For instance, in front of many houses one finds something like enormous clay tubs; that is where the family sleeps, at night, at flood-time, in order to avoid the scorpions which the water chases out of the fields. I do not know what the weather has been like in Cairo these days, but though I was on donkey-back, I was almost as hot as I am in Cairo in the summer. I believe it hardly ever rains here. Excavations are still in progress in the Valley of the Kings, and a host of little Arabs are employed in them; they form a chain, and they sing. They are very agreeable, and irrepressibly gay; I saw some amusing ones this evening, leading herds of donkeys or making camels go at a fast trot.

One returns from the Valley of the Kings to the cliff opposite Luxor by crossing a fairly high pass; the ascent caused me to lose almost all hope of finding interesting fossils at Luxor—not much more than a big bivalve mussel. Down below, there is a whole collection of fine monuments: first, the Ad-Dier El-Bahari Temple, at the end of the avenue of sphinxes of Karnak, and especially the Ramesseum, or temple of Ramses. In the latter are immense lotus columns, as at Karnak, and also the remains of a granite monolith representing Ramses which is even more enormous than the others; the head is over 2½ yards thick. At some distance, right in the middle of the fields, are the colossi of Memnon, which you will have seen on my postcard to Guiguite. The one furthest to the left is made of a single slab; the second is the famous one of which it is said: "Neither more nor less than the statue of Memnon, bathed in the rays of the rising sun, uttered harmonious sounds . . ."; its feet are covered with Greek inscriptions.

January 8. I conclude my letter at Minya. This evening I am taking the students back for the beginning of term, and I might not be able to finish my letter for quite some time if I did not do so right away.

I left Luxor at 5 a.m. of the 4th, and arrived here at 4 p.m. It was a very beautiful journey, in spite of some monotony, and there were marvelous colors on the desert chains at sunrise. I tried to see the famous temples of Danderah and Abydos from the train, but without success; to make up for them, the country-side was very picturesque. The big fields of thick forage are not cut, but systematically eaten by the cattle, rather as at Jersey. What is interesting here is the variety of the cattle, and it is very amusing to see camels, sheep, gamoosas, cows, goats and donkeys tethered to the same rope. None of them is much used to trains yet; when a train passes, there is often a general stampede; young donkeys and little gamoosas, especially, hurled themselves at top speed across the fields. The birds were less shy; around Girga and Tahta, flocks of kites were succeeded by troops of ugly little white skuas which took flight barely twelve yards from the tracks. All along the ditches bordering the tracks are kingfishers of the large sort (white and black—almost like the lesser spotted woodpecker), as well as plovers whose name I do not know, with reddish brown plumage, black breast and head, white throat and cheeks. Perhaps they are simply golden plovers in winter plumage.

The little residence at Minya is delightful; with its oldish paneling, and its large rooms, it reminds me of Le Rocquet, and life there is family style. Only five priests live there, and they are nearly always on mission in the Coptic villages, from a couple of miles north of here as far as the vicinity of Kena. To do anything here one has to know Arabic perfectly, and French can hardly ever serve. The fellahin are big children, pleasant on the whole, and their hearts are quickly won.

The residence has a beautiful garden of which the star piece is a plantation of fine banana palms which a priest takes care of with as much solicitude as Father Rougane used to devote to

220

his asparagus. These trees bear nearly all the year round, you know. There is also a little creamfruit tree; the fruit resembles an artichoke or a pine cone. They are sold in Cairo a lot, but I did not know what it was. I should also mention a doum palm. This type of palm is rarely found further north, but around Luxor it is quite often to be seen in the fields. The trunk is thinner than that of date palms, but it sometimes grows almost as tall; it is quite lovely as a tree, and it breaks the monotony. Dates, mimosas, tamarisks, ziziphus and doums are, in that order of frequency, the only trees of Upper Egypt.

My stay here has been a very busy one. Apart from Sunday, when I did not move, I spent three days outside. The first and third, I crossed the Nile to hunt for fossils in the cliff of the Arabian desert, which is very close, as you will see from the sketch opposite. The first time I collected a good number of sea-urchins, and flushed a jackal and a pair of large owls. The second time, that is, yesterday, I went further. A good fellow, the owner of almost the whole of the cultivated belt opposite Minya, gave me two of his *gâfirs* (guards), armed with *nabouts* (clubs) and piston guns, and under their protection (fairly useless, I believe, though I am told otherwise), I went far into the mountains. While we were out looking for the *gâfirs*, I would have liked Father there to enjoy the spectacle of an Egyptian farm: good fellahin coming to the master's office to deliver, or receive, piastres, just as in Father's office; a visit to the sugar cane field, for all the world as at Carthelades. Only here there was a whole population of donkeys, camels and Arabs, and I can only compare the size of the field to that of the meadows at Vialle. The objective of my excursion was some old alabaster quarries. There are some at various points along the Nile, and the Egyptians made considerable use of them. The alabaster is in veins and lentils in a layer of calcareous rock; to exploit it, slits were of course dug along the veins, and these gave us a little shade at noon; I was as hot as on the finest summer day.

On the way back, we again flushed a horribly timorous jackal in the cliff, and I found there an enormous slab which the Egyptians had obviously intended for a colossus. It had been sawed away on all four sides, and is still attached to the mountain by the base. On its upper face there is a rough figure of a Pharaoh, probably the sketch of the future statue. To give you an idea of the size, I lay down across the head, my feet on the nose of the profile; it would have needed at least another 20 inches to reach the nape of the neck, by stretching out my arm; so the head was at least 3⅓ yards wide. I do not know whether this slab is known [(yes, it is)], because in order to make out the sketch of the Pharaoh one has to be standing at the right spot, and one does not easily notice it.

On Saturday, I went to the big sugar mill of Sheikh Fadl, to the north. On that day, there was thick fog until 8 o'clock, so that when we wanted to cross the Nile, our boatmen did not quite know where they were. I was going there to see a powerful Bedouin chief from whom I wished to get some information about an ammonite which he had found and given to the father of one of our students. Unfortunately, he was at Suez; I hope I shall be able to see him some other time. I benefited from the expedition in that I saw a sugar plant working at full tilt. From now until Easter, that is, during the cane season, work is at fever pitch. The management is French; among them are very distinguished and agreeable persons. I was particularly interested in the analytical laboratory; at every stage of processing, the juices are analyzed to check the operation. There is a Mr. de Verdal there, from Creuse; you may know the family by name.

I found your various letters here, and last of all Mother's, together with her new year's gift. Thank you very much. I think that a part at least will be for Minya.

Owing to my absence, I have seen very little of Father André so far. He spoke to me very movingly about Albéric; obviously he is deeply attached to his memory. Could you send me one of his photographs? You could simply detach it from one of his boxes and put it in a letter; Father André asked me for one to put in his breviary.

January 9. So I am finishing at Cairo. Yesterday I had an excellent return trip, but you would have laughed to see me gravely eating sugar cane in the midst of my students from Upper Egypt. They all come back laden with chickens, pigeons, and salted fish, and the carriage quickly turns into a stable. At the stops, they buy up tangerines and sugar cane especially, which all the inhabitants simply love. By the way, do you know what the star piece of a banquet is there? A roast sheep, with a turkey inside it, with a chicken inside that, with a pigeon inside that, with a sparrow inside that. It cannot be very easy to carve, but they are not very fussy about that.

Goodbye, I love you and continue to pray hard for you.

Pierre

56

Cairo, January 27, 1908

Dear Father and Mother,

The weather today is the worst one could imagine. Since
yesterday, we have had a violent west wind, with showers un-
worthy of Egyptian skies. Cairo, in consequence, is swimming
in mud, which squads of Arabs are trying to channel into sewer
openings, of which there are very few. In many parts, even this
expedient is nonexistent, and, for lack of an incline, the sidewalks
are bordered by real lakes in which the young natives splash
with delight. The students for their part think it rather fun,
especially because they are sent home two hours earlier.

This downpour came yesterday for the feast of the Holy
Family, the school's patronal day, but all the secular celebrations
are put off in part to Father Rector's birthday (the dinner), in
part to a Friday in February (the Arab play). The religious
solemnity consisted of a Maronite solemn Mass.

One of the special features of these oriental solemn Masses is
that, thanks to interjected prayers, they can go on indefinitely.
(The Coptic Christmas liturgy goes on literally the whole night.)
The Maronite bishop suggested a two-and-a-half-hour Mass to
Father Rector, who naturally asked that it be shortened. It took
about one and a half hours. It must be admitted that otherwise
the ceremony is very beautiful. One characteristic is that the

224

celebrant turns to the people several times to show them the eucharistic species, and he always blesses with a little cross which he holds in his hand. The singing, which continues without a stop, is in purely Arabic rhythm, rather nasal, very guttural, and with scales and musical intervals quite different from ours. The voices of the little choir which came for the occasion were beautiful and well trained. I am getting to like this music very much.

To complete the tale of feasts and the like, Father Mulsant is shortly to give another film showing, which will afford me another opportunity to turn the handle.

As regards classroom life, there is nothing very special; this is the season of fertile monotony of the second term, prior to Shrovetide. Last week I took the science students on the traditional visit to the gas works. Aside from the fact that most of these young men are very agreeable, the advantage of going out with them is that one has interpreters for all the languages of the Orient, and they are many. Every child here speaks at least three languages. I am sorry not to have had an Arab nurse.

Françoise, for once, scolded me too soon; she must have received my answer by now.

By way of scientific news, Mr. Fourtan is drafting a report on my sea-urchins from Minya, and a week ago I brought back from Mokattam half of a vertebra about the size of a head. I only fear that it will not be identifiable.

Goodbye, dear Father and Mother, I kiss you and pray for you.

Pierre

57

Dear Father and Mother,

First of all, I hope that my letter of the end of January (the one with the photographs) finally reached you, for I see from your letters that you are beginning to find my silence a little too prolonged. Yours reach me very regularly, and the last, which arrived this morning, is the one in which Father tells me that it has turned cold again. Here, after the bad weather of two weeks ago about which I wrote you, and which was a real storm, we have as usual had a hot spell in reaction, with a miniature khamsin and a temperature of about 77 degrees. Now we have returned to normal weather, fairly cool on account of the wind which cools off at night in the desert, and does not really have time to warm up again during the day.

On Friday, I saw Mr. de Bélinay, who was taking a roundabout route to Constantinople via Egypt; one of his sons is serving in some government post in Constantinople. His visit brought me a whiff of Auvergne, and I should doubtless have had a much stronger gust had I known on which day Uncle Georges was going through the Canal. To return to Mr. de Bélinay, he came on one of the new extra-fast steamers, and is now at Luxor.

These last two weeks, we have carried on with the regular order. As to what I teach, I am partly involved in organic chemistry, concerning which I had only rather vague notions, so that I have to work quite hard, especially in order to be able to prepare my students. But it is interesting.

By the way, wherever did Mr. Poncet see that I had the supervision of the older boys? Nothing of the sort, and it would have been a sufficiently important event for me not to have omitted it from my letters.

I took my older students to visit the electric power station which is under construction, and which is to supply the future garden cities of the "Oases," as well as the hypothetical metropolitan railroad which would run as far as Suez. In any case, money is no object, and there are superb machines, with turbines of the latest model. The staff were very pleasant; one of the workers had arrived practically the day before from the Saint-Denis plant in Paris, and I gave him his first view of the Pyramids from a roof-top.

Biel wrote me a letter which I received today. I shall try to answer as soon as possible. At the same time, a consignment of fairly heterogeneous Egyptian products is now leaving for Antoing. I hope it arrives safely.

The death of Mustafa Kamil Pasha, which took place yesterday, was a big event for Cairo; he was the leader and the soul of the nationalist party, and and this is a rude blow for it. The funeral must be taking place right now, and is probably an anti-British demonstration. A rather touching detail; some reprieved persons (?) from Denshawai (the village where two English officers perished two years ago, in the Delta) came to weep with their families.

Next Friday, the Arab play will be presented; for me, since I understand nothing, it will be like a repetition of the previous ones—the same audience of tarbooshes, the same costumes, and especially the same intonations. The film showing is next week.

I still go to Mokattam, where the wadis are beginning to grow green again in places; Guiguite will learn with envy that quite nice black buprestids with white wings are to be found on thistles; they are not uncommon, actually. I was also given a migratory locust, which I sent off to Antoing with the other things. I must also have some interesting fossils, which I picked up the day before yesterday, but have not yet examined.

About the prints in *Illustration,* it is true that most of the Pyramids now have steps, but that is only as a result of the removal of their smooth granite facing, which served as building stone, like the materials of most of the temples.

Goodbye, dear Father and Mother, I kiss you and pray for you. My best to Guiguite; I sympathize about her plaster-work!

Pierre

58

Cairo, March 4, 1908

Dear Father and Mother,

As you see, I am writing to you on Ash Wednesday itself, which, with Lent, brings Shrovetide to a close and thereby restores quiet and gives me time to send you my news.

These past two weeks I have led a fairly active life; there have even been three film shows, two here and one at Alexandria, each with its own specific character. The films were a series made by Father Mulsant, portraying scenes of Syria, Palestine and even Egypt, with some reconstructions of the life of the child Jesus. One might have thought that the Orientals would have remained indifferent to scenes of their own countries, but the contrary was true, especially on account of the innumerable Syrians in Cairo who were greatly moved at the sight of Lebanese customs.

The first show was very select, which did not prevent an overflow of enthusiasm about the preparation of the national dish (kubbeh, a kind of barley cake, if I saw rightly); and many among the audience spontaneously clapped their hands in rhythm to accompany dance scenes—it was very typical. The second show was offered free to an assembly of ladies or women (mainly Syrian) who came, of course, with their whole families; the hall was filled to capacity, and in perpetual communication with the Arab priest, who was explaining the scenes. Finally, at Alexandria, the audience, which was smaller on account of the size of the theatre, was much more European. A good gentleman wept his eyes out at the sight of the child Jesus, and a baby tumbled down after trying to climb up on a chair, an operation which resulted first of all in the appearance, on the screen, of a very odd-looking little head with a tousled knot of hair.

Like last year, I operated the projector, not without some apprehension at the beginning of each showing (except the second) lest something might not work. The whole apparatus had to be transported to Alexandria in three sizable packages, and for a time I believed them to have gone astray; I was quite worried.

I was very glad to see Alexandria again, both the people and the places which recall my first contact with the Orient. I had just time enough to climb up on the terrace to see the sea and observe that the *Heliopolis* was not in port. The most remarkable boat was an English cruiser, the *Aboukir,* which had brought the Duke of Connaught (commander in chief of the British troops in Egypt and the Sudan, come on his annual tour of inspection). I stayed only a day and a half, and shall probably make the trip again on the 12th to give tests. I would as soon do the three hours' train journey south as north, but the Delta is beautiful all the same. Everywhere, now, one sees nothing but berseem (*Trifolium alexandrinum*). Every morning, caravans of camels (each laden with about half a wagon load) converge on Cairo from every side, delivering berseem to the different stables; one of them majestically enters the school grounds very morning.

As usual, there was a raffle and some quite amusing stage shows, not to mention the traditional Chinese shadows where a

230

gentleman's head is cut off, to the amazement of the very littlest ones. The program even included an Arabic adaptation of the *Médecin malgré lui;* every native student speaking his own language immediately feels at ease and suddenly acquires an unsuspected wealth and originality of gestures. The gestures are "homegrown," but all the more amusing for that.

Shrove Tuesday is a general holiday; I took advantage of it, as in previous years, to go to the desert north of the Pyramids. I returned with a rich store of sea-urchins and even two starfish, not to speak of a snail caught in the act of feeding on the excrements of a jackal, which will not fail to interest Mr. Pallary very greatly. All along the edge of the desert, near the fields, there was a crop of pretty purple irises with fine leaves like those of graminaceae, which I had not noticed in other years.

I saw Mr. de Bélinay on his return from Luxor; I even went out with him one evening into the Arab quarters. His son is to be ordained at Hastings in August, after which he will preach a little mission in Corrèze.

Mr. du Buysson wrote to me again, very kindly as ever, and asked me for some snails where Hymenoptera had built their nests. I shall try to find some, but so far—that is, in the space of three years—I have seen only one of this type, and that was at Alexandria. That is not very encouraging to investigation.

I did not tell you that Mr. Couyat had hardly arrived in Cairo before he left again for Upper Egypt; for some time he has been exploring between the Nile and the Red Sea (at the level of Kena), toward the Jebel Dokhan (*Mons claudianus*), where the ancients had their quarries of red porphyry. I hope he comes back as soon as possible, but I understand that he likes it where he is.

Goodbye, dear Father and Mother, I kiss you as well as Guiguite; I would be happy, indeed, to learn that she is in better health. I do not forget that the 7th is Albéric's birthday; with

231

you, I shall pray to him to bless us all, and we shall tell our
Lord together that we believe that what he did in taking him
from us was for the best.

I kiss you.

Pierre

59

Cairo, March 27, 1908

Dear Father and Mother,

The news of Guiguite's unhoped-for improvement was a joyful surprise to me; indeed, you must be astonished that I did not express my feelings sooner. I confess that I prefer this unexpected improvement even to some relief obtained at Lourdes. The Blessed Virgin's hand is thus more evident, and it can hardly be ascribed to Guiguite's imagination.

As every year, on the 19th I remembered you all very specially; we have been separated for nine years now, but I am convinced, and you must be too, probably, that in return our Lord will reunite us more closely in heaven, and the price for this is not too high. I do not have to tell you again how happy I am to have taken the path which I did, and how grateful I am to you for making it possible for me to enter upon it.

To come to the local news. On the 12th, as I had told you I would, I returned to Alexandria to test some unfortunate candidates who did not, I think, find me very indulgent. The journey was very pleasant, without the worry of transporting a projector; I was even able to enjoy a view from the train which is not customary in France on account of the arrangement of the trains. In Egypt, the boxcars are in front, and since express trains have no third class, the last carriage is a second-class car with a corridor. One can therefore sit in such a way as to watch the tracks disappear under one's feet, and to observe a vast and fairly stable countryside (even though it is receding). It is far more agreeable, and the Delta, with its fields and its buffaloes, was delightful to see, especially in the evening.

At Alexandria I had time to rush to the port to see the *Cairo* (one of the two new rapid-service steamers). It is really enormous, with six cabin decks, all white, and it must put its rival companies out of business by draining away all their passengers. I do not know whether the Heliopolis Oasis Company, on which it depends, is doing equally good business in Cairo; some rather unfavorable rumors are circulating on that subject. In any case, an automobile race organized in the neighborhood of the "Oasis" on a course marked out in the desert had disastrous results. One car skidded at full speed and crashed into the spectators; there were several deaths, of course. Had it skidded to the other side of the course, the notables, the khedive, and the Duke of Connaught would, apparently, have received the impact. Quite understandably, the papers launched a tempestuous campaign, against the organizers.

Last Monday I saw Mr. de Bélinay again; he had left his niece here, Mlle. de Viviers, whose sister is at the Sacred Heart, and was coming to fetch her. Constantinople did not appeal to him. On the other hand, he greatly enjoyed a walk we took together through the palm woods near Matariya. I am sorry that Father does not know him; he loves the mountains, the woods, the countryside, and his life in his country house in Corrèze is very much like that at Sarcenat. Unfortunately his return journey will not take him through Clermont; otherwise he would have gone to bring you news of me.

The day before yesterday. I had to escort Father de Chabanes as far as Saqqara; he is preaching Lent here. The excursion, though not very novel, was not unattractive. In a field bordering the desert, I saw a flock of light coffee-colored birds, which run like young partridges, but fly very differently from them; Iñes Bey will probably be able to identify them for me without difficulty. To please my companion, I went down the great Pyramid at Giza (on our way home), which is quite an experience, and not a very agreeable one. One has to slide down a long ramp, polished by generations, in a sitting position, then go up another one, just as long, then follow a long passage almost on all fours, and all this to reach a small vaulted chamber, reeking strongly of bats. What I had not anticipated was that the Egyptians had set aside something like slots between two slabs on two sides of the chamber; these are repeated from layer to layer, thus forming an air passage; otherwise the atmosphere would be unbreathable.

Mr. Fourtan was filled with admiration for my fossil asterias; he had to send them to Paris for identification. I also found, in the Mokattam hills, the remains of some very interesting big, flat, sea-urchins, but I cannot manage to find any sufficiently complete ones.

Yesterday was the fortieth day since the death of Mustafa Kamil Pasha. An enormous crowd flocked to his tomb (all the government schools came spontaneously, but without having to miss classes, as on the day of the funeral, since it was a holiday), and there were many speeches. His photograph is sold all over the place.

Goodbye, dear Father and Mother, I kiss you and pray for you.

Pierre

60

Cairo, April 7 [1908]

Dear Father and Mother,

Term is very nearly over, and consequently vacation time is quite close; I am happy to think that your big and little boys will soon be coming back to you, virtually from the four corners of heaven. Mother tells me that you have given up Vialles; does that mean that you will spend the holidays at Sarcenat, despite the rigors of the mountain spring? I was grieved to hear of the death of Uncle Joseph du Ranquet, especially on account of Françoise, and still more about the misfortunes of poor Uncle Cirice; I think the directors of his firm must be in a very poor way, or very foolish, to deprive themselves of a man of such high moral stature—unless, of course, they consider him too scrupulous.

Here, at school, we are in the throes of examination time, as is to be expected; I personally have to deal mainly with the few candidates for the Egyptian baccalaureate (May 11), who are so few that their departure will only slightly affect my routine, in contrast to previous years. A good number of others will stay with me to continue a course (an interesting one, incidentally) until July. I refer to the philosophy students. In science-rhetoric, there is one (!) candidate for the French examination, whom I shall have to tutor until the same date.

Meanwhile, I continue to scour the Mokattam hills in search of my big flat sea-urchins; I have some larger fragments already, but they are still not satisfactory. The day before yesterday I came back with a satchel packed . . . with camel's excrements, populated by big, livid caterpillars, and I immediately sent a boxful of them to Father de Joannis. Guiguite will be interested to learn that I am now at the head of a whole family of desert lasiocampa caterpillars.

I have begun going out with Iñes Bey again. Among other interesting insects, I have seen, for the first time, some live Belostoma, huge water bugs two or three times as big as the *Hydrophilus picens.* Tomorrow evening I am going to the second meeting of the Egyptian Entomological Society, most of whose members I know; I shall tell you about it in my next letter.

Yesterday I went to a meeting of the Egyptian Institute, where there was a rather curious report on a violent storm which raged over the Delta from January 25 to 28. The minimum temperature was only 37 degrees, but the continuous wind and rain, and perhaps other unknown factors too, caused the death of thousands of sheep (in pasture) and of some fellahin.

Mr. Couyat will soon reappear on the Cairo scene. He wrote to me from Aswan, where he has returned from his expedition. The unfortunate side of his affairs is that he returned with a quite bad ophthalmia, but he seems to have recovered from it, judging by the way he refers to it. Anyway, I shall be glad to see him again.

In answer to Father's questions, berseem is used as fodder when it is fresh, and what is not brought into town is cropped on the spot. In the summer, at least in Cairo, horses and mules eat chopped straw. I never see flamingos here; I have not even seen them on Mariut, where they are neverthless quite common, as well as—especially—on Lake Manzala (Port Said). As for the yellow birds of the Pyramids, they are in fact *Cursoiens gallicus.*

I close with wishes for a happy and joyous Easter. The youngsters will probably be there to get their eggs. Please kiss them from me. I kiss you and pray for you.

Pierre

61

Minya, Easter Tuesday
[End of April 1908]

Dear Father and Mother,

Since I did not write to you before leaving Cairo, I am rather behind; but now you have your boys with you, and their presence is of a kind which will make you pass over any irregularity in my correspondence.

Here, first, is a sketch of the last two weeks of Lent. I had left you with the announcement of a meeting of the Egyptian Entomological Society. It duly took place, and was both interesting and intimate. After the reading of a note on desert insects, we began talking, and since there was no lack of friendly members, everything was for the best. The budding society is receiving encouragement from scientists from the four corners of Europe, as well as their (interested? . . .) offers of assistance. What it is to be in Egypt! It must be confessed that its geographical position and its deserts make this country an unusual subject—or rather, area—of study. However, to prove to Guiguite that curiosities are a very relative thing, I will tell her that one of the big entomological events of last month was the capture of a *malthinus* (an insect similar to the telephorid, small, soft, black, with a yellow crescent mark at the end of each wing-sheath). I should add that for the moment it is the only *malthinus* in

239

Egypt, and a new species—nevertheless, the capture is not very impressive.

Mr. Couyat has finally returned from his desert, where he had spent three months alone. He has brought back cases of rocks which I have not seen, a good number of theories, and some ibex heads (. . . *sinaiticus*); this is an animal easily caught by dogs. For the moment he is straightening out his things and treating an ophthalmia he contracted at Aswan.

Holy Week was fairly free of responsibilities for me; I continued to teach the upper classes almost regularly, and this time I did not have to worry about the ceremonies. Finally, in the evening of Holy Saturday, I set off alone for Minya. A fellow entomologist will not be arriving till tomorrow; he will be of invaluable help to me.

Upper Egypt is certainly not the same in April as in January. First, during the past three days the thermometer has risen to at least 89 degrees inside the house (actually, it may be much the same in Cairo; I arrived in a period of south wind). And then, instead of the lush verdure of winter, one sees mostly huge fields of yellowing wheat, short-eared and stocky; it is romantic, but less cool.

On Easter Sunday, I did not move. However, in the morning I was made to pontificate in the role of subdeacon at the solemn Mass; I think Mother would have been thrilled. It was a consular Mass, which the French consul (there is one at Minya, a fine Corsican who lives in these parts) attended in full regalia. You may not know that in these circumstances the Gospel is brought to him to kiss; in general, he is proud of the distinction.

Yesterday, today, and probably tomorrow, my program is as follows: from 7 a.m. to noon, trip to the Arabian mountain on the other side of the Nile; in the evening, rest. In the course of two expeditions, I practically plotted the geological section of the cliff, and collected a good number of fossils. Let us hope that all will continue well. Among my other evening occupations, I can watch the banana trees in the garden, which are in full growth; as there are about 250 clumps, and as the stems grow almost throughout the year, one can see stems at every stage of development, which is rather curious. You know that the banana tree is cut with the stem; but since each stool always has several suckers, it is quickly replaced.

I have received all your letters. I was saddened at the news of the death of Aunt Blanche de Félig. But I was delighted, of course, about the job found by Uncle Cirice. I shall write to you when I get back to Cairo. You will realize, perhaps, upon reading the present letter, that it was written rather at haphazard. That does not stop me from praying for you all and loving you very much. All the best to the boys, if any of them are still there.

I kiss you.

Pierre

62

Dear Father and Mother,

I meant to write to you as soon as I got back from Minya, and now I am a week behind; the reason is that hardly had I arrived than I was caught up in the preparation of a whole series of classes, which left me very little free time. In a week, the Egyptian candidates will take their examination. Furthermore, the program of the science-rhetoricians has to be completed as quickly as possible on account of the French candidate. And, finally, there is a whole group of science-philosophers —future engineers or doctors—who have to have extra physics and chemistry, and also botany. But this workload will be disposed of so soon, owing to the shortness of the term, that I do not feel it much.

The end of my stay at Minya was as happy as the beginning. Every day, without exception, I crossed the Nile to go into the mountains, but only once outside Minya, at Mallawi, further south. And never has an expedition been made so easy for me as was that one. One of the students here, whose family is one of the most important in the region, was waiting for me at the station with mounts and provisions. I had a magnificent donkey which trotted as fast as a horse; a boat was waiting on the Nile. In such circumstances, we soon arrived in the desert.

As at Minya, the right bank is formed of a tongue of cultivated land, well planted with date palms, which is abruptly cut
off by the desert. The cliff is not so high as at Minya, and cut by
several wadis which open on the sandy plains. I made an approximate section of them, and collected a good number of sea-
urchins; then, as the heat increased, we withdrew to a cave, the
remains of an Egyptian quarry. There the provisions made their
appearance, in the shape of a whole lamb, stuffed with rice;
pigeons, also stuffed; and a lot of other things. Fortunately, some
Arabs were there to help us. Only a schismatic Copt, who was
still observing Lent, insisted on refusing to touch so much as a
piece of bread, lest by mischance it might be offered to him by a
hand defiled by contact with meat. This good fellow, a guard
(*gâfir*) from the Department of Antiquities for the area, was
armed with a piston-rod gun, which he loads with big round
bullets; these are weapons which they do not hesitate to use
when the occasion arises.

To sum up, I was quite lucky in my investigations in Upper
Egypt. Altogether, I brought back about six completely new
types of sea-urchins; a note will appear on the subject in the
not too distant future.

You will remember, perhaps, that last year I told you I had
found the sketch of an Egyptian colossus. I had occasion to speak
about it yesterday to someone at the Museum of Antiquities, who
seemed to be very interested. I do not believe that it had been
reported, as I had been somewhat casually informed.

In the Minya desert, I met an old acquaintance—some great
plovers. That did not fail to recall memories of the ringed
plovers of the Allier.

The very great heat at Easter came to an end on Easter
Friday with a strong gust of wind, together with torrential
rain in Cairo. Now we are enjoying the usual fine weather.

Mr. Couyat has returned to Paris, with a number of my

243

crystals; if Biel goes to the Museum laboratories (minerology), he will be able to see them there.

That is my principal news. Mother will be glad, perhaps, to know that I am going to have to say a few words to the students at Matariya, for a sodality pilgrimage. I confess that I prefer giving a class to preaching a sermon, but it is a habit one has to acquire, and one must do something for the Blessed Virgin.

I expect you now have forget-me-nots, primroses, daffodils and the statue of our Lady on a round table, with perhaps the blue china bowls decorated with rams' heads.

Goodbye, dear Father and Mother, I kiss you as well as Guiguite, who will not take it amiss if I do not write to her today. Thank you for her water color, which I placed without any need for explanation.

Pierre

63

Cairo, May 19, 1908

Dear Father and Mother,

We have now reached the period of real Egyptian heat. On Sunday it was about 104 degrees, and since then the thermometer has been over 77 degrees every day. Right away, the lebbeks have put on their leaves again, and are becoming covered with very perfumed balls of flowers. Although it rather hampers my excursion, I quite like this period, and Mother need not fear that the weather tires me.

The events of the past fortnight are as follows: first, the Egyptian candidates took their written examination. The results will not be out for about a week, but the parties concerned appear fairly satisfied, which I must admit is but a mediocre reason to be hopeful.

Next, last Monday, I made a communication to the Egyptian Institute on the geological constitution of the mountain at Minya. I enclose, for your entertainment, a somewhat pompous report on the proceedings, which were very modestly attended, at least numerically speaking. The interesting part, undoubtedly, was Mr. Fourtan's work on my sea-urchins; in the end, there were eight new species (one of which was a *Teilhardi*, of course), two of which constituted new genuses. You see that there is still enough to do in Egypt. All this will be published, and you will probably see it; but the reports of the Egyptian

245

Institute are famous for the time they take to appear. As the newspaper cutting shows you, Mr. Maspero spoke, and really it is music to hear him.

Finally, on Sunday last, I preached the sermon at Matariya which, as I told you in my last letter, I was shortly to give. It all went off very well, and I was the richer by a morning in the country on a very hot day.

Father Rector's birthday is now set for the 31st, as well as the opening of the prize essays. Regular classes are at an end, and anyway a good number of the boys are beginning to leave for Syria or Alexandria to escape the heat.

In spite of all the problems involved, I congratulate Father on retaining his "seat" at Orcines. As for internecine quarrels, I really think the people of the Orient are past-masters in the art. Right now, the Copts are quarreling among themselves, and latterly the Patriarch had to be convened to Rome; fortunately Pius X seems to be an outstanding man who will not hesitate to straighten things out.

To change the subject, somewhat disquieting rumors are circulating concerning the intentions of the natives in the Sudan; supplies are apparently being rushed in. But the area is favorable to red herrings.

Meanwhile, in Cairo, roller-skating is all the rage. I believe that the rink is hardly larger than the terrace at Sarcenat, yet the fans are numerous, to judge by all the students who tell of their exploits. Didn't Miss Beveridge tell us about this sport at one time?

Goodbye, dear Father and Mother, I kiss you. The month of the Sacred Heart is approaching; as the family has many reasons to believe itself especially consecrated to the Sacred Heart, I shall not forget you. If only Notre Dame du Port could restore Guiguite's legs . . .

Pierre

64

Cairo, June 9, 1908

Dear Father and Mother,

This time, again, I believe I am rather behind in writing to you; your letters, on the other hand, always reach me with the greatest regularity.

The past weeks have been marked by a great number of feasts or extraordinary occasions, a situation which is not likely to end before the close of the school year. Ten days ago, we celebrated Father Rector's birthday, with the customary offerings of sheep, wine and macaroni, and the banquet for the faculty. The day before yesterday, for Pentecost, the first holy communion ceremonies took place. Then there are the numerous prize essays which come just at the right moment for sending the boarders to Matariya twice a week to cool off. That is certainly not unwelcome on some days—we have had a very hot end of May, and on the 28th it was 107 degrees near Cairo; usually, at this time, the maximum is between 91 and 95 degrees. But there is an almost constant north wind, which the school receives in full force, and which on the whole makes the heat quite bearable.

The day following Father Rector's birthday, I set off, as usual, to spend a day in the desert beyond the Pyramids. I think I told

247

you before that two hours from there there was a very interesting cretaceous mountain, not to speak of the white and dreary landscape with its exquisitely desert-like flavor. Guiguite will certainly be excited to learn that one can find mylabrids and big julodids on the tufts which grow at infrequent intervals, as well as great carabids, shiny black, with white spots; and graphipterids and anthids, swarming underfoot.

We ran into a large herd of camels, which were particularly interesting because they included a number of camel colts; these are delightful, and with their tousled wool and their bright black eyes they look innocent and good-tempered. By way of palpable finds, I brought back a series of ammonites of iron oxide, which are something new for Egypt. Unfortunately, probably only the genus will be more or less identifiable. They were at the bottom of a sandy depression, which the wind had uncovered just enough to make some of them visible.

The results of the Egyptian examination are now out. Half of our candidates passed, with good marks, but that, out of a total of six, is not very brilliant. One unfortunate managed to fail the oral, which was exceptionally bad luck. In a fortnight, it will be the turn of the French baccalaureate.

I continue to see Iñes Bey and other entomologists quite frequently, and several students here are beginning to show unbounded enthusiasm [for entomology]. At present, our investigations center exclusively upon the lebbek wood, where the young branches are preyed upon by many particularly interesting clerids or bostrychids.

I am glad, for you and the older ones, that the Centrale year is drawing to a close. If only Joseph passes his examination.

I was very amused about Father's meeting with Mr. Glangeaud. Perhaps Biel should get in touch with him? He would get information from him, and take part in some interesting excursions.

Goodbye, dear Father and Mother, I kiss you, as well as Guiguite, and the boys when they come. You know that during this month especially I pray for you all.

Pierre

65

Cairo, June 10, 1908

Dear Father and Mother,

Last night, just after I had sent off my letter, I learned that someone from here, Father Lammens,[1] was going to take a cure at Royat. Of course, I am asking him to go to see you to give you news of me, and he will hand you the present letter. He is a distinguished Orientalist, who will be able to provide Father with a host of particulars about Islam (if that happens to interest him). In return, I think that you would do him a real service if you could give him some pointers to enable him to spend his time at Royat in as interesting a way as possible.

Had I had time, I would have prepared a consignment of insects for Guiguite, and some stones for Biel (I dare not add for Yéyé, who might not be very flattered at this attention, and would probably prefer cigarettes). I had better bring them myself, either this year or next (I still know absolutely nothing about my future destination).

I kiss you.

Pierre

[1] Father Henri Lammens, born at Gand on July 1, 1862, entered the novitiate at Ghazir (Syrian mission) in 1878; he authored many works and scientific reports on Islam and the Near East. He taught for nineteen years at the University of St. Joseph at Beirut, and died there on April 24, 1937.

66

Dear Father,

I am writing to Mother for her birthday; the official letter will therefore be for you, and in any case it will not give you much news of the past fortnight. It has been quite a busy time, but without any outstanding event. We are still alternating between spells of heat (with a maximum of about 102 degrees), and cooler weather (with a maximum of about 89 degrees), each of which continues for four or five days. Father Lammens, whom you have probably seen, left us during a hot spell, and will have described it to you without enthusiasm. But do not forget that the nights are cool. Recently, our last year's colleagues reported from Hastings that the temperature on a Pentecost morning had been 39 degrees, and frankly regretted the climate of Egypt.

We get the daily bulletin here of the British meteorological service, indicating the temperatures from Alexandria to beyond Fashoda (now Kodok). It is quite interesting to follow. The highest temperatures are recorded at Aswan or Wadi Halfa (113, 128 degrees), in the desert regions. At Alexandria, the temperature is often 40 or 50 degrees lower than here, but the humidity there is very unpleasant.

I have moved relatively little of late; but I did take a trip to

251

the Mokattam quarries which netted me a whale vertebra, bigger and better preserved than those I had previously found, or rather, perceived, since in general it is impossible to extract them. Mr. Fourtan seemed to view it with some interest; a visit I paid him took the place of another trip, and was less hot. At his house I looked with due respect at some sea-urchins which had just been brought back from the area around Darfur.

Of course, with my budding entomologists, we have again been perseveringly combing the acacias, but without finding anything new. The famous *Lasiocampa acaciae* are becoming hopelessly commonplace.

When I next write to you, we shall be very close to prize-giving. This year, we are making our week's retreat at the end of July, before leaving for Alexandria. I imagine that about then, and perhaps even before August 15, I shall begin to know what next year holds in store for me. It has probably not even been decided yet; I dare not tell you to hope.

A characteristic trait of the country—I now teach botany to a group of students, but when I get to cryptogams, I have a very hard time obtaining a few specimens; there are no mushrooms (I am not speaking, of course, of moulds), no bracken, and, to get a few wretched mosses, I shall go to a sakieh beyond Matariya. Here, however, in all the ditches, one finds *marsilia,* a plant which Father may know, and which looks much more like a four-leaf clover than like a close relative of bracken. I recall the vegetation of the "chestnuts," for instance, as very luxuriant.

Goodbye, dear Father, I kiss you as well as the boys who are with you; now I come to think of it, they may all be there by now, except Gonzague.

Pierre

67

Dear Father and Mother,

Now I am a week late in writing to you; I meant to write at the beginning of this week, and then a host of very different occupations obliged me to put it off until today.

First, on Wednesday, we had prize-giving, preceded for some days by the sorting and selection of books for the various boys, which takes a considerable time. The prize-giving itself was unspectacular. It takes place in the courtyard, outside, in the shade of those large tents with multicolored geometrical designs which adorn every Arab celebration. The most curious moment of the ceremony is right at the very end, when people are already leaving. At that point, all kinds of persons come up to the dais with requests; I can still see a very small Copt answering to the unfortunate name of Jean Gress coming up with piteous eyes, pushed by his older sister. Like many others, he did not understand why everyone should not be granted a reward on this day of joy. I consoled him with a multicolored alphabet. Others would like a book for an honorable mention, etc. Then the tears flow. An odd thing is that paper crowns are highly prized.

As for my weekend, it was taken up with two trips; I deliberately make many of them, not without some melancholy, because I am much less sure than Father that my fate next year will not be to pace the cliffs of Hastings.

The first time, I went to the pebbly undulations traversed by

253

the ancient Suez route. I saw there, once again, a pair of *Certilauda desertorum* which were hardly shy at all, and I again found some small myrmecophilous insects which I had first come across last year, and which probably constitute a new species (by the way, there is still another sea-urchin *Plagiocidaris teilhardi:* that is the name which has been bestowed upon a species brought back last winter from Abu-Roach). The afore-mentioned insect is approximately this shape, and lives in swarms among the debris of insects heaped up by ants.

Yesterday I went to Wadi Hef, which winds through a deep canyon through the main group of mountains north of Helwan. I consider it the most beautiful region in the Cairo area. You go up a dried-up bed completely leveled by the torrential winter rains, between high, table-form mountains, which often end above the wadi in a sheer cliff. In the wadi there is a relatively varied flora. I again saw a small caperbush very common at Minya, which curiously enough was covered with splendid, fire-colored chrysalids. I collected a number for Mr. du Buysson. But I wonder why these insects, which are usually found only in isolation, had gathered on this bush. The debris left by the water furnished me with three interesting types of shells, which had perhaps floated down from far off, for I have never seen any live specimens. There was also the trail of a varan, whose feet leave prints like a child's hand; but these creatures are hard to come across.

Now as to my program for the coming month: on Wednesday, we go into retreat, which closes on the 31st; then, on the 3rd, to Alexandria for our vacation; and afterward . . . ? I shall write to you early in August. Between now and then, I shall not fail to pray for you all.

Goodbye, dear Father and Mother, I kiss you as well as Guiguite, Biel, Yéyé, Joseph and the Marneffe people.

Pierre

68

Sidi Gaber, August 6, 1908

Dear Father and Mother,

First of all, I still have no information as to what I shall be doing next year. It will be announced on the 15th, and you can imagine that in any case I shall write to you on the same day.

And now, you see from the letterhead that I am on vacation for the third time. I am writing to you on the shores of this very beautiful, though rather banal Mediterranean, and I still have another ten days or so to observe it. As I told you, the last days in Cairo were taken up in a salutary way by the retreat, a period which is more useful than entertaining. I did not forget any of you, or little Loulou whose birthday has just passed. At the end of those austere days, we joyfully took the road to Alexandria, and here the hours go by gaily because many of us here have known one another a long time. In particular, there is a young Father Soury-Lavergne here, whom I mention because Father may know the name; he has an enormous family, and they live in the Plateau Central region. At the end of the month he is taking a steamer for Madagascar, and I think he is very fortunate to do so.

In the absence of fossils, of which there are absolutely none, I collect shells for Pallary, but not on the beaches. I comb the reeds and brackish waters of Mariut, at great damage to my clothes, and I have already picked up two species which had escaped me last year. Yesterday, I was able to go to my favorite region, that is, the desert adjoining Lake Mariut, west of Alexandria. This time I got as far as Hammam, about forty miles away, in the khedive's ineffable little train. The Bedouins —the men in small fezes and white burnus, the women with their heads wrapped up in something resembling multicolored turbans, and wearing filigree sashes—are much more like Algerians than Asians. As for the countryside, at this point when the barley has been cut and the soil plowed up, it is absolutely dreary. Some tents, a few buildings near stations, and then, as far as the eye can see, a stony terrain, undulating, strewn with round, dark green clumps of a kind of rosemary. Somewhere in that area stands the ancient convent of St. Menas, which Father probably knows by name. On this excursion, my principal find was a pretty little helix which I did not know, and various Coleoptera discovered under stones. In spring, when the flowers are out, the place must be teeming with insects, as evidenced by the wing-cases of two species of julodids. At the moment there are only black-beetles, akis, pimelea, stenosis and Curculionidae. The fauna is very Mediterranean in character, less African than in Cairo. But it's a change. To assess the value of what I have picked up, I have to see the Cairo collections again.

This morning I received a letter from Robert du Buysson, telling me among other things of his brother's admiration for Biel's research.

And now, goodbye until my next letter, in a week's time, which will put an end to all uncertainties. I kiss you with all my heart, as well as Guiguite and the boys.

Pierre

Cum permissu Superiorum.